1984
In Memory and Imagination

1984
In Memory and Imagination

Personal Essays and Short Fiction on the 1984 Anti-Sikh Riots

Edited by Vikram Kapur

AMARYLLIS

AMARYLLIS

AMARYLLIS

An imprint of Manjul Publishing House Pvt. Ltd.

• 7/32, Ground Floor, Ansari Road, Daryaganj, New Delhi 110 002

Website: www.manjulindia.com

Registered Office:

10, Nishat Colony, Bhopal 462 003 - India

Distribution Centres:

Ahmedabad, Bengaluru, Bhopal, Kolkata, Chennai, Hyderabad, Mumbai, New Delhi, Pune

ISBN 978-93-81506-91-2

This edition first published in 2016

Printed and bound in India by
Replika Press Pvt. Ltd.

To my parents, Brigadier HL Kapur and Satya Kapur, who gave me the gift of free thinking, in loving memoriam.

Contents

Introduction *ix*

In Memory

1984: An Overview 3
Kirpal Dhillon

November 1984 24
Ajeet Cour

Stone Games 42
Rizio Yohannan Raj

A House of Lies 59
Hartosh Singh Bal

A Question of Identity 74
Preeti Gill

Why Not A Collective Cry For Justice! 86
Humra Quraishi

When Steel Entered My Soul 96
Rana Chhina

In Imagination

When Big Trees Fall 109
NS Madhavan

The Perished and the Saved 126
Jaspreet Singh

The Morning After 138
Mridula Garg

Trilokpuri 156
Vikram Kapur

Dried Apricots Smell Like Dead Fish 172
Pratyaksha

Among One's Own 185
Harish Narang

Karma 197
Aditya Sharma

About the Contributors 225

Acknowledgements 231

Introduction

LESS THAN A month after the mayhem following Indira Gandhi's assassination on 31 October 1984 had died down, my friend Sarabjit Gujaral visited me at my home in South Delhi. Sarabjit and I were as thick as two friends can be. We sat next to each other in class, hung out together on weekends, and frequently visited each other's homes. I don't remember much about our conversation that day, which meant it would have been no different than what it usually was; genial and packed with the kind of stuff boys in their teens obsess over – sports, cars, girls… though maybe not in that order. The tornado of political violence that had hit our city recently would have figured nowhere in it.

What happened after Sarabjit left has stayed with me for the past three decades. In those days our security guard or chowkidar was an ex-army havildar, a Rajasthani with a closely cropped white head, a walrus-shaped, salt-and-pepper moustache, and a tall, erect bearing. No sooner had Sarabjit gone than he came up to me and said with a grim face, 'These days you should keep your distance from Sikhs, baba. They are no longer good people.'

At the time, those words merely made me marvel at the extent to which the world had changed in a short span of time. A few days had transformed a Sikh from a go-getting super-patriot to a bad character synonymous with sedition and murder. The mere sight of a beard and turban was enough to induce the taunt of ugarwadi or terrorist, and turbaned Sikhs, invariably, received 'special attention' from the security forces. Before the year was out, the words of another Sikh friend would illustrate how vitiated the social and political climate had become. We were travelling in a local DTC bus, when I asked him to dispose a dirty paper napkin out of the window. His response was to inquire, in all seriousness, 'Are you sure you want *me* to chuck this?' He then explained himself with the words, 'These days whatever a Sikh throws becomes a bomb.'

I cannot recall what I said or did in response to my chowkidar's 'advice' all those years ago. I certainly didn't follow it; Sarabjit and I are friendly to this day. That said I didn't take any strong exception to it either. I'd remember if I had. Most likely, I said or did nothing and went back to my room. There would have been some uneasiness about my friend being painted in an unsavoury light. But it was far too mild to matter. Certainly the full implication of the chowkidar's words did not dawn on me—not that day or the next or the one after that. It was seventeen years before I figured that one out.

On 11 September 2001, a day better known as 9/11, I was living in Seattle. That morning Islamic militants hijacked commercial airliners and flew them into the twin towers of the World Trade Center in New York. That single act transformed everyone with a brown face into a potential troublemaker in the eyes of many Americans. Two days after 9/11, at an academic conference, an African-American colleague summed up how much the world had changed in that one day with the words, 'Now the cops ain't gonna stop me. They gonna stop you.'

Until 9/11, the only time I had felt like a minority in America was while filling out the race section of an official document. Unlike blacks and Hispanics, Indians were comfortably anonymous in the America of the late twentieth century. The fact they did not figure on the radar of the American mainstream, while rendering them obscure, protected them from overt racism. Furthermore, I inhabited the liberal and diverse world of university campuses and literary gatherings, where everyone went the extra mile to be seen as open and inclusive.

9/11 changed all that. Suddenly, I found myself being viewed with hostility by perfect strangers. Even with good friends, relations entered a different realm. There were times during conversations where I could sense some of them wondering, He seems okay but… Getting on to a flight was an ordeal. As a young, brown man, I fitted the profile of a potential terrorist to a T, which meant me and my baggage were subjected to all kinds of searches. My white American girlfriend, unable to handle all this crap, broke up with me. The fear I might end up at the wrong end of a hate crime was never far from my mind. I stopped going out at night and frequenting places where I was not known. Before 9/11, I had been a cheerful, outgoing person. Now I turned inwards with a vengeance; I became isolated, morose and, as the days passed, increasingly angry. It was a smouldering anger, the kind that does not rise to the surface but continues to eat away inside like a killer infection silently working its way through your bloodstream. Looking back now, I don't know what would have happened if I were not a writer. Writing provided an outlet through which my hurt and anger could escape on to the page. Without that facility, who knows...

It was then that I figured out the full import of my old chowkidar's words all those years ago. As Vikram Kapur, and hence on the right side of the divide that sprang up in India in 1984, I did not have the faculty to figure out what was going on inside Sarabjit or, for that matter, any Sikh any more than my white American friends could appreciate what I was going through. Sarabjit probably understood that and, for that reason, donned a genial mask in my presence that told me nothing of the deep sense of hurt he had to be feeling. And even if he had shared it with me, chances are, I wouldn't have understood it in the least. Back then, I had no idea what it means to wake up one morning and find yourself cast as the other; a role that has traditionally belonged to the Muslim in independent India. It took my American experience to apprise me of that.

The violence and political grandstanding get all the headlines. But for the ordinary citizen, the true implication of being on the wrong side of events such as Indira Gandhi's assassination and the anti-Sikh pogrom that followed is to face up to the reality of life in a society that sees you in terms of a series of derogatory labels while revoking the respect and dignity due to you as a fellow human being. That is reflected in a number of writings in this anthology, with some writers going on to compare what happened to the Sikhs in 1984 to what the Jews faced in Nazi Germany.

A lot happened in 1984. A sitting prime minister was assassinated for the first time in Indian history. The three days of mass murder that followed saw 2733 Sikh, men, women and children being massacred, according to official estimates. Senior Congress leaders presided over the bloodletting which radicalised thousands of Sikhs who wouldn't have had anything to do with secession or the Khalistan movement in the normal course of events. While the mayhem was unfolding, the organs of state designed to protect the citizenry – the police, the government and the administration – sat about and did nothing. In some cases, their functionaries even participated in the looting and killing. And the prime minister of the day, Rajiv Gandhi, who was also the slain prime minister's elder son, sought to explain everything away with the now infamous statement, 'When a big tree falls, the earth shakes.'

The tragedy of 1984 is not behind us. As recently as 2012, Lieutenant General Brar, who led the troops during Operation Blue Star, the Army raid that sought to expel the militants holed up inside Sikhism's holiest shrine, the Golden Temple, on 3 June 1984, was attacked in London for his role in that operation. In 2014, the Punjabi film *Kaum De Heere,* based on the lives of the men responsible for Indira Gandhi's assassination, a direct result of Operation Blue Star since she was the person who ordered the Army raid that led to the desecration of the shrine, was banned. To this day the struggle goes on to deliver justice to the victims of the mass murder following the assassination. Rather than entering the garbage heap of history, the 'corpse' of 1984 continues to show signs of life. It has become a testament to the Nobel Prize-winning American author William Faulkner's words: 'The past is never dead. It isn't even past.'

This anthology seeks to examine all aspects of the tragedy of 1984 by combining nonfiction pieces with fictional stories. While nonfiction probes the changing psyche of society by scrutinising the factual history of the times, fiction catches the horror of what happened by giving the human story a number of unforgettable faces. There are pieces that zero in on that moment in history. Others remind us of how it continues to fester in the lives of several people to this day. And still others view it in terms of its ramifications for Indian politics and society.

One of the functions of the written word is to force a culture to remember. It is only through remembrance that the lessons of the past are learnt and a better future secured by not repeating past mistakes. When it comes to a passage of history, such as the events of 1984, remembrance is crucial. The biggest reason the Jewish holocaust that occurred during World War II will never be repeated is because the world has not been allowed to forget it. Silence is hardly the panacea for the grave crimes of history. Silence not only leads to forgetting, but allows the guilty to escape unscathed. Collective amnesia and getting away with murder are a vitriolic mix guaranteed to play out the tragedy all over again.

For a long time, we in India sought to forget 1984 by dropping a stubborn shroud of silence over what happened. Perhaps we believed, naively as events have proved, that the way to recover from it was to not talk about it. As a consequence, 1984 repeated itself across India in the nineties and beyond. The anti-Sikh pogrom that occurred then was nothing short of the state making war on a section of its citizenry. Various incarnations of that have been seen in India since then.

The celebrated Urdu poet, Mirza Ghalib, wrote: 'Lest we forget:/It is easy to be human, very hard to be humane.' The events of 1984 are, if nothing, a testimony to human baseness where the desire for revenge and an obsession with narrow religious identities trumped the egalitarianism on which a democratic, pluralist India is based and without which it cannot succeed. That, however, is not possible unless we rise above the baseness seen in 1984 and embrace the humaneness to which Ghalib refers. Certainly India needs just as generous a dose of it now as it did in 1984. It is my hope that this book will strike a blow for that cause by showing just what happens when a society goes to war with a part of itself.

Vikram Kapur
New Delhi
July, 2016

In Memory

1984: An Overview

Kirpal Dhillon

AS AN ARDENT LEFTIST, I found the growing cynicism among many of my favourite writers with regard to the doctrine of communism in the post-World War II years deeply disturbing. These counter-narratives would later impel me to seriously engage in study and research into the morphology and mechanics of state tyranny and despotism in its various forms. The catastrophic events of 1984 in India, though contextually far removed from the post-war European milieu, do nonetheless epitomise the conceptual and functional make-up of an autocratic and oppressive state. The cumulative after-effects of the grievous events of 1984 in India would last for decades and the ensuing frictions and fissures in social and political terms would continue to seriously damage the institutions of governance and their dynamism. The circumstances that led to such a change of direction in an India that alone stayed firmly committed to a liberal and democratic system of governance under Jawaharlal Nehru, India's first prime minister, even when most post-colonial societies were opting out of the democratic mainstream, needs to be examined circumspectly to find answers to many baffling questions that have agitated people since the traumatic events of that year.

It seems to me that the incremental slide of Indian democracy into monocracy under Indira Gandhi, Nehru's only child, who became prime minister two years after his death in 1964, is the key to understanding the phenomenon. I consider 1984 and all that it symbolises as a defining moment in Indian history, marking the beginning of the end of a caring and compassionate administration, nurtured so lovingly by her father. Regrettably, all subsequent regimes would fail to reverse this unwelcome trend.

In a hugely diverse and vast land like India, which is home to many disparate peoples, some sub-national groups are sure to harbour grouses of various kinds against the central authority for historical reasons alone, as in India's remote Northeast. They also intensely resent being denied their rightful share in the new power structure at the national level and are prepared to fight for it, if need be. Anti-state restiveness and insurgent movements remained confined to the Northeast and the primarily tribal lands of Central India, with mainstream India remaining largely unaffected, until the 1980s. That is when the strategic and mainstream state of Punjab got seriously embroiled in a horrendous militant upsurge. It would take over a decade for the Indian state to bring it under some degree of control though the bitterness and antipathy generated by a series of untoward events would, in turn, spawn several other problem areas for the political leadership to manage. Of late, rightist Hindu groups seem to have turned overly assertive in claiming primacy in the country's political and administrative sphere, despite a hoary secular tradition among them that spawned and nurtured the idea of a pluralist and inclusive India, as defined by Sunil Khilnani in his landmark work, *The Idea of India*. This could itself be responsible for creating a deep sense of insecurity and unease in India's many religious, linguistic, ethnic and cultural minorities. While Muslims and Christians started feeling alienated from the Indian polity a few years after Nehru's death in 1964, it would take the traumatic events of 1984 for the Sikh people to fully realise the dilemmas faced by minority segments in an India where the principal majority community appeared intent on reneging on its famed pluralist heritage. The two key events that would notably turn the miniscule Sikh minority into a deeply troubled and alienated community were Operation Blue Star in June 1984 and the Sikh pogroms in Delhi and elsewhere some five months later. The ensuing hurt and outrage in the small but well-regarded and influential Sikh community was indeed deeply unsettling and the pain and agony of the horrors of 1984 would remain a searing memory.

My appointment as Punjab police chief on 3 July1984 placed me at a vantage point where I was both a close observer of a series of very disturbing events, pursuant to the Army intervention in the state, and an active participant in helping resolve some very grave issues that arose therefrom. Apart from my normal charter of duties as the police chief in a strategic border state, I was also, I was told, a part of the *healing process*, designed to soothe the hurt and anger among the Sikh people due to the abrasive conduct of the troops during Operation Blue Star in the Golden Temple, Sikhism's holiest shrine, and Operation Wood Rose in the countryside. I am unsure though whether the *healing process* was indeed a prime ministerial initiative or just another buzzword, coined by the Intelligence Bureau or IB sleuths and home ministry mandarins, to create a smokescreen that put off addressing the many complex issues thrown up by some misconceived and badly executed Army manoeuvres.

The *healing process* charade was dumped by Rajiv Gandhi, Indira Gandhi's son and successor. Rajiv went on to win a landmark three-fourths majority in the general election, early in 1985, by portraying the Sikhs as a treacherous and anti-national community that had taken to terrorist violence against the Indian people. He promised to rid the nation of such lawless elements, thereby, perhaps, indicating his future approach to the problem of dissent and disgruntlement among many minority segments in this heterogeneous nation. Soon after the elections, he pulled out the just-elected chief minister of Madhya Pradesh, Arjun Singh, and dispatched him post-haste to Punjab as the governor. Singh's abrupt removal from MP would stir a whole lot of rumours, mostly unflattering to him. It is important to mention this as it would significantly affect his performance as the governor of a crisis-ridden Punjab. In a political party like the Congress, for long a Nehru-Gandhi fiefdom, it is of the utmost importance for the lower-rung leadership to get back in favour with the family as soon as possible. Arjun Singh, therefore, set a rather tight schedule for somehow *resolving* the so-called Punjab problem and thus demonstrating his superb administrative and political expertise to the supreme leader. That his ill-advised and short-sighted policies would lead to an alarming escalation of Sikh militancy in India for the next several years became amply clear soon after he left the Punjab Raj Bhawan later that year.

In retrospect, it is obvious that all the tragic events following Operation Blue Star—Indira Gandhi's assassination, the Sikh massacres in Delhi and elsewhere, the so-called Rajiv-Longowal accord, the assassination of Longowal, the Akali signatory to that ill-conceived and badly drafted document, and the ensuing intensification of Sikh militancy in the country—cannot be viewed except in a cause-and-effect relationship. Nor can they be delinked from the after-effects of the policies pursued by Singh as the Punjab governor, then under presidential rule. As Operation Blue Star forms a key link in the chain of events that would cumulatively result in gravely denting the political and administrative vitality of a strategic border state, it is important to highlight how the Sikh leadership was gradually pushed into playing a dicey game of one-upmanship, first with the Punjab Congress and then with the Union government. Notably, no Sikh agitation, from the Gurudwara movement in the early 1920s to the Punjabi Suba agitation in mid-1960s, ever turned violent or explicitly confrontational. Why then did the 1980s agitation take such a gory turn? That is where an obscure but flamboyant religious preacher, heading an ancient Sikh seminary in Punjab, Sant Jarnail Singh Bhindranwale, comes in.

Around the mid-1970s, Punjab Congress leader Giani Zail Singh prevailed upon Sanjay Gandhi, Indira Gandhi's loutish son, to latch on to Bhindranwale in a sinister plan to steal the religio-political thunder of the long-time political voice of the Sikh people, the Shiromini Akali Dal or the SAD. Now enjoying the patronage of the ruling party in Delhi and its top leadership in Punjab, the maverick Sant soon took to criminal intimidation, plunder and murder, obviously in order to undermine the credibility of the SAD leadership. When arrested in a murder case by the Punjab police, Zail Singh, then Union home minister, had him released. Bhindranwale's fast-growing clout in the Punjabi countryside, as well as in local administration, had the Akalis seriously worried.

They tried to upstage him in order to seize the political initiative, first by approaching the Union government with a list of *demands* and then periodically launching morchas or sit-ins where, among other things, they blocked roads and railways to pressurise the authorities for the acceptance of their *demands*, standard practice among Indian politicians. Bhindranwale, still enjoying Congress party patronage, was increasingly taking to violence and terrorism for the same purpose. That roughly was the background to all the alarming developments that would ultimately make Army action inevitable and probably acceptable to a large segment of Indian political opinion.

The desultory course of the government-SAD talks was manifestly indicative of the official apathy to wind up the negotiations any time soon, apparently in a bid to build a national consensus in favour of a military operation to oust Sikh militants, hiding in the Golden Temple complex, led by Bhindranwale and his associates. Among them was a former, highly-decorated Indian Army general with a formidable reputation for strategic and tactical expertise. Bhindranwale's sermons grew more strident by the day and his followers struck freely in the Punjab and elsewhere, allegedly assured of protection and support of the Congress party and the Union home ministry. Such an environment provided an ideal opportunity for Bhindranwale's followers to substantially expand their operational span to cover most of North India, including Delhi. Young Sikh men and women came to implicitly believe in his sermons that vociferously highlighted the many allegedly unjust and inequitable policies of the Indian establishment aimed at humiliating the valiant Sikh people in order to finish them off as a proud community with a glorious history. While driving through the Malwa countryside in

April 1984, I found large groups of highly agitated young Sikhs gathered around sound systems relaying the fiery speeches of Bhindranwale that blatantly castigated the Delhi establishment or *Dilli durbar* and the prime minister, whom he contemptuously referred to as that *Brahmin woman* or *Bahmanan di kudi*. This sentiment would grow phenomenally all over rural Punjab in the months leading to the Army action on 3 June.

The SAD was then led by a triumvirate of a mild-mannered Sant Longowal, a tough-talking GS Tohra and a shrewd but discreet PS Badal. Such a marked attitudinal variance among the trio could not but gravely undermine their capacity to provide quality leadership to their deeply disturbed people. Nor could they devise a judicious strategy to meet the dual challenge of a reckless militant leadership and a manipulative Congress party impatient to oust the Akalis from the Punjab political landscape forever. Notably, of the trio, only Badal would survive to claim the entire legacy of that fateful interlude in Sikh history.

When all their morchas and sit-ins failed to move the Union government to address any of their demands, the SAD declared a grain-roko morcha or stop the movement of grain from 3 June. This would, incidentally, become the key argument for the Army to defend the launching of Operation Blue Star on 3 June, a patently flawed argument as we shall see later. By now, almost the entire mainstream media and political parties had come to largely accept the government position on the worsening Punjab situation that was being carefully highlighted by the government-controlled media. For some time, Hindu political lobbies, too, had been clamoring for a major Army intervention.

Finally, the Indian Army launched a major operation on 3 June 1984 by laying siege to the Golden Temple in Amritsar and several other gurudwaras all over Punjab. Its stated and specific objective was to flush out Sikh terrorists, who had turned the holiest Sikh shrine into a veritable fortress. According to PC Alexander, who had served as the principal secretary to Prime Minister Indira Gandhi, in *Through the Corridors of Power:*

> It was the proverbial last straw. The Akalis declared on 23 May, 1984 their intention of intensifying the agitation by calling for stoppage of movement of food grains out of Punjab as well as a refusal to pay taxes and other charges from 3 June. This call was a virtual invitation to anarchy, which the state police would have found impossible to handle in addition to having to cope with the daily (heavy) quota of killing, destruction of government properties, looting of banks and other crimes. It was immediately after this call by Longowal, on 25 May to be precise, that Indira Gandhi finally made up her mind to summon the Army. She sent for General AS Vaidya—the army chief—and asked him to keep the Army on alert as the civilian authorities may require its help to deal with the situation in Punjab.

This contrived attempt to obfuscate the many critical issues directly impinging upon the future course of history in a strategically vital state, which were then under discussion with the Akali leadership, fails to own up the periodical roadblocks put up by the authorities, as if by design, to derail the talks.

After Operation Blue Star failed to normalise the Punjab situation, Alexander tried to impart a convenient spin to a Central initiative that had gone horribly wrong and would, in fact, seriously aggravate the militant sentiment and violence, not only in the Punjab but also in some far-off areas. Notably, this operation was the only one of its kind in modern Indian history. The only other Army manoeuvre that was to hurt the public psyche as intensely as Operation Blue Star was the Jallianwala Bagh massacre ordered by Brigadier General Dyer in 1919, incidentally also in Amritsar. But that was the act of an imperial power, determined to effectively, if brutally, suppress the rumblings of a revolt in a subject nation. Operation Blue Star, on the other hand, was mounted by Indian soldiers in a free and democratic India against its own people. Moreover, though Operation Blue Star, and other military manoeuvres for that matter, started off as pure and simple Army operations with the entire civilian bureaucracy, including the district magistrates and district police chiefs all over Punjab, barred from discharging their legitimate and rightful duties, they were later sought to be passed off as acts in *aid of civil power.* This became necessary when many uncomfortable questions cropped up regarding the disposal of cases pertaining to thousands of people detained by the troops during and after the operation and kept in military custody in the Amritsar cantonment behind barbed wire, not unlike POWs, thereby violating basic legal provisions that do not allow detentions beyond a certain duration, except under valid judicial remand. Also, such custody can only be either in a police lock-up or a notified jail. Thus, the detention of such a large number of people in places, other than duly constituted jails, without a proper judicial remand, was patently violative of law and procedure. These critical flaws needed urgent attention.

Firstly, the army action had to be *ex post facto* authenticated by the state home secretary as stipulated by the relevant rules for Army *aid to civil power*. Executive magistrates had to be coaxed and cajoled, often with great difficulty, to sign remand warrants in back dates and a part of the cantonment, where the detainees had been lodged, was formally declared a *jail* with retrospective effect. General Gowri Shankar, the Punjab governor's security advisor, and I had to fly several times to Amritsar to sort out the mess left behind by Operation Blue Star. Among several questionable acts of the Army establishment was the choice of 3 June as the D-day to kick off their operations. 3 June was also the martyrdom day of the fifth Sikh Guru, Arjan Dev, where thousands of Sikh men, women and children were gathering in the Temple complex to pay their homage to the Guru and were sure to get caught in the melee. No wonder, civilian casualties in the operation far outnumbered those among the terrorists. Furthermore, the Army authorities apparently failed to carry out a proper identification of the dead bodies. In addition, they were unable to appropriately account for all the deaths in the operation and arrange autopsies as soon as possible, as laid down in law and procedure. Completion of all legal formalities would have effectively forestalled all derogatory references to statistical fudging. It remained unclear whether they did not sufficiently appreciate the legal position or were engaged in deliberate prevarication. The troops also allegedly set fire to the Sikh memorial library, which had stocked precious manuscripts and memorabilia of great historical value, some dating back to the Guru period. Furthermore, there were reports of executions by firing squads of groups of people with hands tied behind their backs, as reported by Khushwant Singh in *The Punjab Story*.

Interestingly, a key issue regarding the timing and operational efficacy of Operation Blue Star and other central government actions during those critical times, which was hotly debated by the Delhi chatterati, was why the establishment let the public order situation in Punjab slide into chaos and anarchy before choosing to address it through Army intervention. Furthermore, was Delhi, in fact, preparing the ground for an Army strike to decisively put an end to Sikh aspirations for political pre-eminence in the only state where they formed a slender majority? Or, in a larger context, was the Army action in Punjab a prelude to and a sounding board for similar manoeuvres in other areas facing dissident movements in a climate of growing unrest and discontent among the many minority and disaffected groups demanding, *inter alia,* more clout in administrative decision-making within their traditional cultural and linguistic *homelands*? Since the Army intervention in Punjab proved to be disastrous, no subsequent government would resort to such a disastrous venture again for a long time to come.

However, coming back to Operation Blue Star, the Indian establishment continued to insist that it was the unexpectedly heavy-armed resistance from the militants that made the use of heavy armour within the Temple complex unavoidable; this they ascribed to lack of intelligence from the state police, the most convenient whipping boy of the Indian establishment. In fact, there was plenty of actionable intelligence as the Punjab CID had set up a sizeable presence in the city as well as inside the Temple and was *operating* a number of very reliable sources. A Punjab CID superintendent of police practically lived and worked inside the Temple complex throughout those critical times and was regularly feeding valuable tactical and strategic information to the CID headquarters in Chandigarh through written and telephonic reports; information that was routinely shared with the concerned Army authorities. By virtue of his long posting in Amritsar and the nature of his duties, the officer enjoyed an excellent but discreet rapport with many senior Akali and Congress leaders as also those within the militant groups. If the Army chose to launch an operation of such magnitude on the basis of inadequate data, as claimed by their spokespersons, it can only be ascribed to their failure to carry out thorough surveys and reconnaissance sorties before finalising their operational plans as required in such situations. It was possibly the famed Sunderji swagger that must have played a major role in selling a seriously flawed operational plan to a trusting General Vaidya and a skeptical but somewhat over-awed prime minister. Besides, the latter could now afford to sit back and watch the turf battles, between the Akalis and Bhindranwale, boil over and open a window of opportunity for the faction-ridden Punjab Congress to put their act together and win the next election, whenever held.

I had interacted with General Sunderji fairly closely during the periodic civil-military liaison meetings in Shimla and Chandigarh. He was a tall, handsome, well-informed and charming officer, and he knew it. All these attributes were custom-made to also inculcate in him a high degree of intellectual arrogance. Later, as the Army chief, he inveigled Prime Minister Rajiv Gandhi into embarking upon the disastrous Sri Lanka venture, arguing that a show of military prowess was essential for achieving regional supremacy. In the case of Operation Blue Star, he was probably able to get past his chief by building a rapport with the PM by outlining a plan of operation that provoked little opposition, precisely because of its incredible simplicity. Briefly, it envisaged the use of Army commandos to swiftly seize Bhindranwale and his close associates and neutralise the militants in the thick of the night, without causing any damage to the buildings. The operation was to start after the *Guru Granth Sahib* was taken to the Manji Sahib for the night, as per tradition (*maryada*) and would be over before it was re-installed in the Harmandir the next morning. Any tell-tale signs like bloodstains, etc., would have been swept clean before the devotees started gathering the next day. No one would even know that any untoward event had taken place. Apparently, either Sunderji had placed too much confidence in his commandos, or had grossly underestimated the strength and ardour of the militants. In both cases, it was indicative of poor leadership and inadequate appreciation of the situation. Operation Blue Star did, of course, succeed in eliminating Bhindranwale and his principal aides hiding in the Akal Takht, although a significant number of his followers managed to flee because the troops had failed to properly secure the numerous exit points from the Temple complex. Also, Bhindranwale and his militant rhetoric, which had earlier left the bulk of the Sikh community unmoved, acquired much more acceptability after his death. An amazingly large number of ordinary Sikhs refused to believe that he was indeed no more. Myths and legends would soon grow around him and it would take years before his ghost could be exorcised. Operation Blue Star also caused deep outrage and unrest among Sikh troops in some Sikh regiments, fanning mutinous conduct. Sunderji remained impenitent and unapologetic until the last about the calamitous Operation that he had led. In addition, Operations Blue Star and Wood Rose and other Army manoeuvres in the Punjab set off a chain of catastrophic events, not only locally but nationally, with Mrs Gandhi's assassination being the most tragic and ruinous.

Operation Wood Rose, an adjunct to Operation Blue Star, that was supposed to clear the rural areas of militant elements, was to prove even more counter-productive, because it was spread over a far larger area and the command structure was more diffused. It involved a string of *siege-and-search* operations in the villages in which the troops would lay siege to the target village early in the morning in preparation for conducting house-to-house searches for possible militant presence. Village life in India centres round extensive morning activity. Siege-and-search operations, that blocked all movement during a very important part of the day, causing immense distress to the villagers, were deeply resented. Also, as the search operations were primarily meant to screen young people, the latter would often flee the village. Later, many of them would cross the border into Pakistan and it wasn't long before the latter realised the immense potential of the situation; the resentment and distress among these young Sikhs could be exploited for subversion and worse. Many of these young Sikhs would later return to India, indoctrinated, armed, trained and motivated by Pakistan, to set off a most deadly phase of terrorist violence in the country. The insensitive conduct of the troops during Operation Wood Rose towards the peasantry and even battle-scarred veterans with distinguished military backgrounds would authenticate widespread rumours in the rural areas that suggested the Indian state and its Army were engaged in a planned manoeuvre to destroy the cultural and spiritual heritage of the community. All this would significantly contribute to fuelling a most lethal militancy in the country that would take a toll of thousands of lives, while damaging the institutions of civilised governance and alienating a whole generation of Sikhs.

A profoundly painful collateral damage of Operation Blue Star was the destruction of the Akal Takht, the most sacred of the four Sikh takhts or centres of temporal power, along with its many holy relics. The sanctum sanctorum of the Harmandir, too, could not escape the fury of the Army firepower. This was perhaps inevitable in an operation of the kind the Army launched in the Golden Temple, although a better-planned manoeuvre might have achieved the operational goals without causing so much destruction and bloodshed within the holiest of Sikh shrines. Even months after Operation Blue Star, Sikh men and women could be seen gazing dolefully at the scars left by the assault and reverentially caressing them in a deeply troubled state, as if they were mourning the loss of a loved one. Akal Takht occupies a unique position in Sikh tradition. For, it was here that the sixth Sikh Guru, Hargovind, assumed both the spiritual and temporal leadership of his people and raised a militia to fight the tyrannical rule of the Mughal emperors and their proxies in the Punjab. Over the centuries, it had become a symbol of resistance by armed force, if necessary, to injustice and oppression, providing a focal point for the community to meet and choose an appropriate course of action when faced with adversity. That could come in various forms in an environment of insecurity and fear at the hands of an autocratic and brutal state structure. Historically, Operation Blue Star happens to be the worst disaster to befall the Akal Takht in over two centuries; the last time something like this occurred was in 1764, when the Afghan raider Ahmed Shah Abdali had it razed to the ground. As a rallying point for a community in distress, the Akal Takht has served both as an inspiration and an opportunity to re-organise and fight another day. The destruction of the Akal Takht and the desecration of the Harmandir would act as a strong unifying force for all the different shades of opinion and social segments among the Sikh people. Later, the Army action in the Golden Temple, viewed as patently sacrilegious by the Sikhs, would become the most convincing argument the militants would employ to win over support in ample measure.

While the grave after-effects of the Army intervention in the Punjab were not unexpected, Delhi and its neighbourhood, too, were fast sliding into disorder and chaos. The IB reports regularly alluded to the deepening of extremist sentiment in the Punjab while warning of reprisal attacks on state entities and prominent Hindus. It was important that we in Punjab kept a close watch on events in Delhi and its adjacent areas for any tell-tale signs of a Hindu backlash against growing extremist violence. The worsening public order situation all around led to suggestions that the Army be re-deployed. However, I opposed the move as it seemed to me that the very presence of the troops, blamed for the desecration of the Golden Temple, would hinder rather than help in battling lawlessness and militant violence. The then governor, KT Satarawala, endorsed my view. Having resisted the suggestion of Army re-deployment, I was well aware of the heavy responsibility that I and my officers now carried to fully secure the state against the growing stridency of sundry extremist groups and rabble-rousers out to take advantage of the mounting unrest in the Punjabi countryside. In this endeavour, my officers were unwavering in their commitment to contain and eliminate terrorist violence at all costs. Fortunately, neither the state government, then under presidential rule, nor the Centre interfered in our areas of responsibility and we were doing fine until Arjun Singh landed in Chandigarh in March 1985, replacing the levelheaded and upright KT Satarawala. But that is another story.

The news of Mrs Gandhi's assassination by her Sikh security guards flashed on my office ticker early on that fateful day. The inept and indiscreet manner in which the sad event was projected on the government-controlled television network, showing explicit visuals of unruly mobs of infuriated Hindu men shouting highly provocative slogans such as 'khoon ka badla khoon se lenge' (we will avenge blood with blood), was clearly against the fundamentals of law and order management. We never highlight any incident or event likely to inflame partisan passions to forestall any adverse fallout. Surely, Delhi could not have been ignorant of the likelihood of a ruthless and violent reaction among the Hindus to Mrs Gandhi's assassination by her Sikh security guards. It was not a good portent nationally, but for us in the Punjab it was doubly so. We seemed to be in for hard times as we now had to battle not only the growing Sikh militancy, but also the likely violent reaction locally to Sikh killings in Delhi. We immediately put in place several tried and tested measures in order to forestall any public order crisis in the Punjab, consequent to mob attacks on Sikhs in Delhi and elsewhere, soon turning into a vicious orgy of killing, arson and plunder.

The carnage outside Punjab was ruthless and well planned, with Congress leaders directing the rampaging mobs. The principal targets of the killing gangs were poor and disadvantaged Sikhs, living in many resettlement colonies, set up long ago by a more caring government, though upscale neighbourhoods did not remain unaffected. Sikh households in mixed colonies were carefully identified with the help of electoral rolls, not unlike the Nazi pogroms against the Jews half a century earlier. The police simply vanished from the scene or, in many cases, even facilitated the success of the assault, later somewhat sadistically labelled as 'teach-the-Sikhras-a-lesson-they-will-never-forget'. And indeed, the lessons, as well as the lesions, of 1984 would never fade completely from the collective Sikh consciousness.

More so, because the killer gangs and their leaders were never brought to book for their monstrous crimes. It is not as if all sections of the Hindus were complicit in the carnage. The first commission to inquire into the horrendous events of 1984 was, in fact, set up by Delhi's Hindu citizens. Chaired by Justice Sikri, a former chief justice of India, it would do more to expose the murky happenings of those dark days than any of the official panels appointed by subsequent administrations.

The magnitude of the Sikh killings in Delhi and elsewhere deeply riled the Sikh community. As overt protests or agitations were banned under the stringent laws in force, they expressed their resentment in religious gatherings all over the state as ordained by the Gurus. Since their political leadership was either in confinement or stood disgraced and enfeebled, it was the militant groups that occupied the centre stage to whip up Sikh sentiment against the establishment. By and large, we were able to forestall any major fallout of the gruesome events in Delhi by meticulously monitoring the unfolding events outside the state and rigorously ensuring the maintenance of public order inside. It was not easy to keep the seething resentment among the Sikh people under constant watch. But receptive management of the many grievances of a deeply disturbed community proved immensely effective in keeping the peace locally. Delhi was thick with rumours of Sikh reprisal killings in Punjab though not a single such incident occurred until much later. By then the entire situation had changed significantly. An acute sense of mistrust deepened among Hindus and Sikhs as the atrocities against the Sikhs mounted across India, especially in states under Congress party rule. In Madhya Pradesh, a Sikh inspector general of police was shifted out as the police under his watch were not doing enough to ramp up the killings of Sikhs. Congress party functionaries considered it their bounden duty to heap atrocities and insults on the Sikh people in order to adequately establish their fidelity credentials with the apex leadership, then vested in the slain prime minister's son.

Even though the IB had a strong presence in the state, I considered it prudent to strengthen the Punjab CID camp office in Delhi. I would also often call up the Delhi police control room to verify reports received from other sources. All in all, the public order situation in Delhi did not seem to be too sanguine. The Indian state seemed to have withdrawn protection to its Sikh citizens. While they had been told to deposit their licensed weapons with the police, Sikh policemen were withdrawn from field duties and Sikh officers remained deployed in staff jobs. When I called the Delhi police control room to help rescue my nephew and his wife from a flat in an upscale colony, under siege by a rampaging mob, RS Sahai, a young Sikh deputy commissioner, who remained posted in the control room all through that critical period, updated me on the situation there. Scores of Sikh policemen, I was told, their beards and long hair forcibly trimmed by lawless mobs, remained stranded in the control room. My nephew and his wife had to be smuggled out of their locality in true filmi style with his hair let loose like a woman, and escorted to the airport to board a Chandigarh-bound flight.

It does not take too big a leap of imagination to recast the past or link the 1984 Delhi carnage with similar episodes in Sikh history, such as the ghallugharas or the organised massacres of Sikhs during Mughal rule. Together with Operation Blue Star, the 1984 Sikh bloodshed contributed significantly to the sharpening of separate identities and agendas between Hindus and Sikhs worldwide, despite the two communities having much in common in social and familial terms. They would henceforth look at every major event, starting with Operation Blue Star itself, in a sharply antagonistic manner. While the Sikhs began to see themselves in terms of a marked minority, not unlike the Muslims, most Hindus viewed Operation Blue Star and its outcome as an affirmation of their primacy in the national decision-making process as the dominant majority. The Sikhs also developed a deeper insight into the problems faced by Muslims and other minorities in a polity that was fast losing its historical and constitutionally-mandated secular character. Having suffered two brutal jolts to their sense of exclusivity, first at the hands of the Indian Army during Operation Blue Star, and then by Hindu mobs some five months later, the Sikhs felt deeply mortified and could not help but look back to history to construct a response in keeping with their past experience of defending themselves against what they perceived to be an oppressive and unjust state. In the process, the pre-Operation Blue Star rhetoric of a dead Bhindranwale acquired an added lustre to galvanize the entire community into assuming a confrontational stance.

Operation Blue Star and its after-shocks also critically ruptured Hindu-Sikh relations, placing the two communities firmly on opposite sides of the fence. Barring a few exceptions, Hindus were generally supportive of the Army action in the Golden Temple, while the Sikhs viewed the action as an outrageous and blasphemous act intended to destroy the self-respect and integrity of the panth. The Operation was widely hailed by Hindus in Delhi amid widespread rejoicing and distribution of sweets, an unsavoury triumphalist act that some Sikhs would reciprocate in equal measure a few months later when Indira Gandhi was gunned down by her Sikh security guards. I was an uneasy witness to a loud expression of glee at a dinner in a classy Delhi colony, where all the guests other than myself were Punjabi Hindus, on the day Bhindranwale was killed in Operation Blue Star. Married to a Hindu, I was aghast to discover that I was no longer a cherished guest at her relatives' homes after Mrs Gandhi's assassination. It was as if I was the *killer.*

November 1984

Ajeet Cour
Translated from the original Punjabi
by Satjit Wadva

THOSE WERE BLACK DAYS, BLOODY days, full of a strange fear of death. A choking sensation rose from the earth to the sky, like a black cloth smothering all.

It was the month of November. The beginning of the month. The year was 1984. The city had been in shock, stunned, since 31 October. The woman who had ruled the country for so many years, the woman who had launched an attack on Harmandir Sahib in Amritsar like Abdali, the woman who had treated the country as her private property, that most exalted empress had been assassinated.

Of course, assassination is deplorable. Reprehensible. Particularly of that woman who had several sensitive layers in her soul too! The woman with large eyes which seemed to announce that she was in control of the universe, the woman with pretty little feet and nimble hands, the stunningly beautiful and intelligent lady who made friends with Castro and any American president with equal ease, the empress of her times.

But in this country, it has not been uncommon for kings or queens to be assassinated.

Here a king often imprisoned his own father, murdered him, chopped up his own brothers, and then proceeded to rule the country.

This country also saw the assassination of the man who was popularly known as the Father of the Nation, a secular nation.

But after any such assassinations, death did not hover over the defenceless and innocent citizens of the nation.

This time, in the Black November of 1984, people were being killed openly, out in the streets. Hundreds of people, instigated and guided by their leaders, roamed the streets and by lanes of the city, shouting slogans. Hordes of people hunting for men of a particular community, and slaughtering them. Raping their women on open streets with their children looking on in dumb awe!

Homes were looted, burnt. People slaughtered.

All this had happened before too. Exactly like this. When the father of this empress had agreed that this country be partitioned, cut into two, and that too with a blunt knife. Then, too, a savage madness had the people in its grip. Then, too, homes had been set afire, like now. Then, too, people had knives driven into their abdomens. They were disemboweled. Their intestines, pulled out of open gashes, lay in blood-soaked puddles, or were scattered on the naked roads, in the fields, and on footpaths.

Then, too, fear, like a vulture, had hovered, and circled over the cities and the villages.

Today, thirty-seven years later, the same thing was happening all over again.

I had closed all the doors and windows of the house, and

sat inside with my daughter, Arpana, on 31 October, and the first three days of November.

Our neighbours destroyed the nameplate hanging on the gate downstairs. They telephoned to reassure us, 'Don't worry. We are here to protect you.'

But when thousands were being murdered in the colonies across the Yamuna, it was not possible to remain locked up, like cowards, in the house.

It had been announced on the TV and on the radio that the Army had taken charge of the law and order situation in the city. But if the Army was guarding the city, how would we be able to leave the house? We would have to cross the bridge over the river to get there. Surely, we would be stopped. They would ask what business we have there...

We would try. We would see how far we could get. We could not remain holed up, cowering inside, while people were being killed on the streets, their heads bashed with iron rods, drenched in petrol and set on fire, alive. Being burnt with kerosene-filled rubber tubes and tyres around their necks. Their homes torched.

When women were being smoked out of burning homes and sexually assaulted right there, next to the bodies of their sons and husbands. Right there on the streets, covered with blood and mud, these atrocities were being committed.

Entire crowded bastis were being devastated. Already in the grip of death and poverty, there was no recourse for them.

In the midst of this murderous outrage, to think only of our own safety was immoral. Unethical.

On the TV and the radio there was a constant replay of the last words of the slain empress: '...Every drop of my blood... Blood!...Blood!...Blood...!'

We, my daughter Arpana and I, set out from the house. The driver was a bold neighbour named Manoj, a Hindu, and I felt that his being a Hindu would prove to be a protective shield for us.

That year the winter seemed to have set in early. We decided to take some food with us – packets of tea, sacks of sugar, milk powder, and some blankets. We turned towards Azad Market to get the blankets because that is where the thick army blankets were available in abundance.

As we were about to turn into Paharganj from Chitragupt Road, right in front of the Paharganj Police Station, we saw a large mob shouting in frenzy. The slogan they were raising was: 'Khoon ka badla khoon!'

As our car crawled past this crowd, I felt choked as though a lump of ice was stuck in my throat.

This was terror!

A primeval fear!

The fear of death!

A numbing fear that my daughter, sitting beside me, could be dragged out by the hooligans….

Having got the blankets, we crossed the bridge across the Yamuna. We saw no soldiers, nor any police. There was no official there. Nobody in uniform!

Nor could we see any turbans. There was no Sikh out on the road.

Proceeding slowly, we reached the Gandhi Nagar School. A police truck was parked outside the gate, and there were two or three policemen relaxing in it, drinking tea, gossiping.

Inside the gate, there was a flood of humanity. So many people! All of them huddled inside the school building! So tightly packed that a needle couldn't have gotten through. Terrified, they stood in stunned silence. They were crowded in tight bunches, filling all corners, crammed in that dust-laden space with their backs to the walls.

Women, children, men, and old people.

It seems someone deep in the crowd recognised me. He raised both his arms, and in a tearful trembling voice said with a heartrending wail: 'Bibiji! Not puddles of blood! Now there are wells filled with blood.'

Perhaps he had read my article 'Puddles of Blood' after the attack on the Golden Temple.

Hardly five months had passed since then. And now....

There was no room for the car, but they insisted: 'Bring the car inside, just inside the gate. Who knows what will happen outside! Someone will set it on fire....'

They squeezed closer together, everyone shrinking back perhaps an inch, till there was enough space for the car.

What amazing people! They had lost everything themselves and yet they were concerned for my car.

We unloaded the car. They said: 'There is no need. The langar is constantly going on. We have enough to eat. You shouldn't have taken the trouble....'

Behind the school building, in what used to be the playground, huge fires were burning under large choolahs. On one, daal was simmering, and on the other rotis were being made.

'But how do all these provisions get here?'

'Oh! There is one Kishenlalji. Morning and evening, he brings sacks full of daal and atta. All the shops are closed. But they say he begs or borrows, or just breaks open the locks of shops and brings the stuff. We have to survive somehow... and there must easily be ten or fifteen thousand people here! Kishenlalji has taken it upon himself to see that we have enough food.'

Human beings were being slaughtered, but humanity still survived.

In the playground field at the back, some fifteen or twenty badly wounded persons, mostly with burn injuries, were lying on the bare, dusty earth. Only one person had something under him – his wife's dupatta. She, herself, her head uncovered, sat huddled next to him, hugging her knees to her chest, sobbing.

In the morning, these people had been taken to a hospital in the police truck but the hospital authorities had refused to admit them saying, 'Those hooligans will burn our hospital down.' 'Those hooligans' meaning the attacking mobs.

There were some with severe burns on their legs and arms. Others had their heads crushed, and yet others had broken limbs. It was a terrifying sight. There was a strange sense of helplessness. A shocked, numbing fear. An abject resignation.

We came back to Connaught Place. Bought bottles of Dettol, bandages, tubes of antiseptic creams, and returned to do whatever we could to clean and dress their wounds.

And then, for the first time, I felt a revolting stench in the air as the wind changed direction. Obviously all these people, having been cooped up like chickens in a basket for so many days, had to relieve themselves somewhere. The building was enclosed from all sides apart from the gate which was open, but no one had the courage to go out.

This was a ghetto! This is how those Jews must have lived, hiding like frightened rats from the atrocities of the Nazis, and taking refuge collectively in derelict towns in Poland and elsewhere. Terrified of death, they had sought shelter in underground sewage pipes, or in man-hole tunnels, or in deserted attics.

When it became dark, we left that place to drive straight to Khushwant Singh's house. It was 9.30 p.m. No relative or friend was allowed in Khushwant Singh's house at this time. His home was closed for visitors after 9 o'clock.

But this was a day of doom. On this day all rules and laws had broken down.

Khushwant opened the door.

I don't cry in anyone's presence. But that night the shock of the whole day, the helplessness, the fear, the horror, they all poured out of my whole body, shaking with tears of heavy grief. Heavier than any burden human endurance can carry! With my head resting on his shoulder, I sobbed loudly, helplessly. And Arpana silently wiped her eyes with her dupatta.

I told Khushwant everything. He listened in stunned silence. I suggested to him, 'Next to the Gandhi Nagar School building is the building of Shyam Lal College. All schools and colleges are closed. If you can speak to the lieutenant governor and ask him to get the college premises opened, these thousands of people will get some space to sit, or even stretch out.'

Khushwant said he had been trying to reach the governor for three or four days. But in those days, whether it was a minister, a police officer or any government official including the governor or the president of India, all one would get was a standard response: 'Sahib is not available.'

Those days no one was available, anywhere. No one seemed to exist. The secretaries repeated like parrots, 'Sahib is not available. Gone for a meeting.'

And that was the truth. The whole country was caught in the eye of a storm. A swirling, black whirlwind.

It was not dust that the wind whipped up, but blood.

The sun had vanished. And the sky itself was hiding behind a bloody veil.

'I'll try again,' Khushwant said. 'I'll phone again at night. I'll call his residence. Can they possibly do anything worse than what has already happened? And what do I have to lose? For two days I took refuge at the Swedish Embassy, with my entire family. We returned home today because the government announced that the city has been put under Army rule, and nothing will happen now.'

'The Army? We didn't see any signs of the Army the whole day! Hardly a furlong away from the Gandhi Nagar School, a mob killed twelve people! We were witnesses. Helplessly looking on from a distance. And something must have happened in Paharganj too, because a bloodthirsty mob had collected there. We passed by them. We crossed the Yamuna Bridge four times and there was no military anywhere. Take care of yourselves! Keep the doors and windows closed.'

It was about 2.30 that night when it occurred to me that an extremely nice doctor, a top cardiologist at the medical institute – Harbans Singh Wasir – was the personal physician to the President of India, Giani Zail Singh. It doesn't matter how blinded a person is because of his rank and position, or how weak, he cannot ignore his doctor.

So I called Dr Wasir. 'Please tell Gianiji to at least get Shyam Lal College opened for these refugees. And, Harbans, if possible, please ask him to get fifteen or twenty temporary lavatories built. And the same number of cleaners... Let them at least dig pits in the ground. There is a real risk of cholera breaking out. Can you send an ambulance there? Some people are wounded. Just lying there in the dust with open wounds.

They could get gangrene! The wounds can certainly turn septic.'

I don't know whether it was because of Harbans's efforts or Khushwant's influence, but on the third day the rooms of Shyam Lal College were opened, temporary lavatories were built, and the cleaners were also deputed.

For the wounded, Harbans sent not only an ambulance but also a team of doctors.

Some artists, social workers, and theatre people came together to form a group. They would meet early in the morning in Lajpat Bhawan, which was a central collecting point for food, clothes, shoes, blankets and quilts. They would sort them and send out vans with the provisions to different make-shift camps in the city.

Arpana and I joined them too. The group worked systematically, and the service and help they rendered was therefore more effective.

None of these people was sentimental or emotional. They were motivated by a deep compassion for their fellow human beings. They didn't weep or cry like me. They were like soldiers in battle. Leaving the comfort of their homes, away from their loved ones, they were committed to the common cause of safeguarding humanity from the onslaught of barbarian bloodthirsty hooliganism.

The gates of Shyam Lal College were opened. The rooms were also unlocked. But no one was willing to go there, leaving the safe haven of the school and stepping out into the narrow street between the school and the college. To step out into that street was to step into the dark kingdom of death, to be at the mercy of the murderous mobs. It meant inviting danger. It meant walking into a seething cauldron of trouble.

What a strange time! When people were petrified to go out in the street, just outside the place they were huddled in!

'Let's break down the side wall of the Gandhi Nagar School, and make a corresponding opening in the side wall of the college, so that people don't have to cross the road,' I suggested.

'But the police...?'

There were two policemen sitting on the raised platform under a tree in the back yard of the school. I took them aside and spoke to them. 'We have to do this! How much money will you want?'

They hesitated slightly. They didn't speak for about five seconds, and kept looking at each other. 'But what if the school and college authorities object later?'

'Don't worry about that. It is my responsibility to have both the walls repaired.'

I paid them. Then they asked, 'What if you don't get them fixed?'

I showed them my Press Card and also gave each one my visiting card.

'Do me a favour. The police truck that is parked at the gate... please park it at the head of the street. We will close the gates of both buildings. Should any attackers come, they will have to come from the lane and you will be guarding the opening there. Then there won't be any danger.'

I knew very well that in those days the biggest danger was from the police itself, because every bloodthirsty mob was accompanied by a protective unit of police. It was in such police jeeps that jerry cans of petrol and kerosene were carried to those settlements where the mobs set people on fire and burnt down homes. Many policemen, too, were among those who looted and raped.

In fact, in some places the police had gone in first and collected all arms – mostly kirpans and, occasionally, a revolver or gun. They said that it was in the interest of keeping peace. When the people had thus been disarmed, the screaming mobs attacked.

The massacres were done in the style of Ghengis Khan or Timur, within the knowledge of the police and with their blessings.

But what blessings? They said these were the orders they had received 'from above'! But then in this country there is always a reward for any favour done. From the constable to the minister, from the peon to the prime minister, everyone dispenses favours to those in need, and collects their own share. Showering favours! And grateful thanks given for every such consideration!

These attacks were different from the attacks of earlier times – whether Ghengis Khan, Timur or Nadir Shah. Those people were fired by personal ambition. They were conquering kingdoms, expanding empires, extending their territories – even though they, in the pursuit of glory and victory, marched through rivers of blood.

These attacks now merely displayed naked savagery, and were proof of their own basest beastliness.

In the depths of my being, I felt historical memories being revived. These attacks, these murders, were like those committed by the Nazis, methodically, and in cold blood. Armed with lists of names, they would ferret out the Jews. They would pull out people – men, women, children who hid like mice – from gutters and manholes, and separate them on the basis of their usefulness. And then send them to concentration camps and gas chambers accordingly.

Six million Jews were murdered.

And today, when I write after years of the bloodbath of November 1984, hundreds of thousands of people are being killed in Bosnia, Sarajevo, Rwanda, Iraq, Afghanistan. It has been going on for years.

And in my own country, the blood-soaked pages of Bhiwandi, Malyana, Gujarat, Mumbai, flutter before my eyes, the pages of which history will always be ashamed.

Punjab and Kashmir, and Assam and Bihar – everywhere it is overcast with dark red clouds of blood.

And the soul-shuddering memory of Nagasaki and Hiroshima still makes our hair stand on end.

Man, the supreme creation of God! In whose heart the barbaric animal is still alive, screaming for blood!

Anyway, the walls of the school and college buildings were broken to give those people a little more space. Even so, there were still about fifteen families in each room. They spilled over on to the verandas, and into the open compounds as well.

For almost a month, Arpana and I stayed there from morning till midnight.

On the seventh day, Mother Teresa's missionaries brought tins of milk powder and biscuits for the women and children.

They spent the entire day, day after day, feeding the hungry children and tending to the sick.

On the tenth day, a tent was pitched. And a short, fat man, an officer of the government, occupied it. Half a dozen policemen hovered around him day and night.

The first thing he did was lock our store room – the room in which we kept the things we ourselves had bought, or collected from friends, relatives and neighbours. Things like blankets and quilts, stocks of food and medicine.

We got to know of this at nine in the evening, the time when we would go from room to room and distribute blankets and quilts as required. It was done very systematically. First lists were made. Then blankets collected from the store would be distributed. Groups of workers were in charge of separate wings. Each one of them was responsible for taking care of the refugees in his wing.

When the lists were ready that night, we went to the store to find it locked and an armed policeman guarding it.

'Who has locked this?' I asked in shocked surprise.

'Sahib has,' the sahib's agent said arrogantly.

'Sahib? What sahib?'

'He joined duty today. He is a government sahib,' he offered casually.

'Where is he?'

'Find out from his office.'

'Where's the office?'

'There, in the tent.'

In the tent, two armed policemen were relaxing, their legs stretched out, resting on a tabletop, as though they had come to a wedding party.

'Where is sahib?'

'He must be somewhere here!' They replied nonchalantly, as though to say, 'Get lost!'

'Here, where?' I was beginning to get angry, and a little bold, too, because some of our people had also reached there. They whispered in my ear, 'Be careful! These sons of bitches can be nasty, they could also throw us out. Those who get people killed can do anything.'

'All they can do is kill. So, a few more will get killed!' I was furious.

I shouted: 'Tell us where he is. He is not in the camp, we have just been around it.'

'Then he must have gone for dinner. It's dinnertime. He has to eat, doesn't he?' one of them snapped back.

We waited for two hours for him to return. When he came, he was chewing paan and reeking of liquor.

'Are you the in-charge? The new in-charge?'

'Yes. I am!' he thundered at us.

'And where were you till eleven o'clock?'

'I'm not answerable to you,' he replied in English.

'No. You aren't answerable to anyone! You are the government. The government is.'

'What do you want?' he snarled.

'Why have you had the store locked?'

'Why shouldn't I lock it? I am in charge of this camp.'

'That's obvious. With all the security you have for yourself! You must be a senior officer. Have you inspected the camp? Have you done any good to anyone? Have you registered a single complaint, a report? Have you appointed anyone to trace the missing members of any family? Nothing! All you have done is to lock the store! And you have come after TWO hours, chewing paan!'

'I'll have you arrested for insulting a government officer.'

'Yes. Why not? You can arrest me, you can get me liquidated – in jail or outside. I am fully aware of your power. You can do what you want, but right now unlock the store.'

'The store will NOT be opened!'

'The store will definitely be opened, and NOW!' I retorted and produced my trump card – my Press Card. 'Here. You can note down my name and address. Arrest me whenever you want. But first open that lock. Not even a pin there belongs to the government. Everything in it has been bought by our own money. Money earned by our own labour, not bribe money!'

He looked a bit shaken as all this went on in front of his subordinates. He had the lock opened, but said softly, 'I'll see to you later.' It sounded both like an embarrassed reaction and a threat.

In this camp, there were ten to fifteen thousand people who had ten to fifteen thousand stories to tell. And there were as many stories from the camps at Trilokpuri, Uttam Nagar, Shahdara and their adjoining colonies. I will tell you only three of them.

One woman sat in the corner of one room, her four children huddled around her. Whenever we urged her to go to the langar for her meals, she would simply shake her head.

'Food for the children? Milk?' The response was the same dejected 'No'.

One day passed. Two days. Three days went by.

By that time, she was no longer sitting. She had sunk to the floor, lifelessly, helplessly. Her children clung to her legs and belly, digging their knees into their stomachs, their heads drooping.

'She doesn't eat, nor does she allow her children to eat. What should we do?'

We brought in people from other rooms to find out if anyone knew her. Perhaps someone from her own colony would recognise her. At last we found one man, who went and sat next to her and talked to her: 'Bibi, get up. Have courage. You are not the only victim… everyone has been hurt.' The woman opened her eyes a little, and then started crying uncontrollably, loudly, helplessly.

'Let her cry. If she cries, only then will she be able to see her children. If she cries, only then will she think of feeding them.'

Then that man told us that on the night of 2 November the mobs had attacked her colony.

'They had dragged her husband out into the street, hit him with iron rods and then put petrol on him and burnt him alive. His shrieks pierced holes in the sky. Her eldest son remained inside, hiding behind a big tin trunk. She took the other children and ran out into the street. The neighbours pulled her and her children into their home and hid them.

'The mob then set fire to her house. She was frantic and tried to open the door again and again. '"Where is my Sohan? Let me go! Let me go and get him, they'll butcher him."

'When the mobs departed, shouting in victory and intoxicated with glee, the neighbours brought all of us, including this woman and her children, to this camp.

'She had gone in the middle of the night to her house looking for her son. Smoke was still coming from the house which looked like a gaping hole, burnt to ashes.

'In the compound she found Sohan's half-burnt body. She thought that the dogs would find it and eat it. So she spent the rest of the night pulling down the remains of half-burnt doors and windows, and tried to burn the corpse of her son.

'We heard of this later when our neighbours told us she had gone to them to borrow kerosene oil and matches.'

This poor woman pulled out bits of half-burnt wood to cremate the body of her half-burnt son! What else could happen to her?

The woman continued to sob uncontrollably. We brought water for her. She drank it. We put a plate of food before her. She broke a morsel with her trembling fingers and put it in her youngest child's mouth.

I'll tell you the second story.

In the verandah sat an imposing, handsome, middle-aged man and his family. Next to him was his pretty, plump and impressive wife, and a young son whose hair was cut like grass. This is the sardarni's story.

'The factory was burnt. The house was robbed and then burnt. The neighbours hid us. When they brought us to the camp they begged me: "Bibiji, save your son's life! Cut his hair." So I cut his hair with these, my cursed hands.'

She wept bitterly.

Then wiping her tears with her dupatta, she continued.

'The factory and the house don't matter. The Guru bestowed them, and He has taken them back. He knows best. He will look after us. He will grant them again. But Kaka's locks! Haaye! How I used to take care of them. Washing them with fresh curd. So beautiful, so thick, so silky. Such lovely golden brown hair!'

The third story is about a very old man who sat in one corner of the verandah. He had sat there for almost a week. Sometimes he would doze off leaning against the wall, his mouth slightly open, his white beard quivering as he shivered with cold. His eyebrows were shaggy and white. He was wearing an old kurta pyjama and his head was bare, covered with white hair.

We tried talking to him but he kept his eyes closed. At times though we could hear a soft murmur, 'Waheguru. Waheguru.' And he would sigh.

We found out that both his sons were auto-rickshaw drivers. They hadn't come home for two days. When his colony was attacked, he brought both his daughters-in-law and their children to the camp somehow, hiding and running to evade the attackers.

After two days the daughters-in-law left, saying they were going to look for their husbands.

'And the children?'

'I don't know whether they've taken them along, or left them with somebody. How to find them in such a crowd?' And his voice faltered.

At that moment I thought of Daarji, my father. If he were alive, he, too, might be sitting in a corner, just like this. His white beard would be trembling just like this old man's. I thanked God that he had passed away before he could see all this.

'Bapuji!' I touched him gently, 'Please take this blanket. It is cold.'

'No. Give it to a needy person.'

'But what if you catch cold and get fever?'

'It will be good. I have nothing to live for.'

I left the blanket next to him anyway. The next day, it was exactly where I had put it. We tried our best but he would accept nothing, neither clothes nor the blanket.

On the seventh or eighth day, I took a white turban for him. For a minute, he looked at it. Then he looked at me. I don't know what it was about that look, but I felt a searing heat. Even now, sometimes at night, I feel it shooting through me.

He accepted the turban with trembling hands. Slowly he unfolded it and, crumpling the width of it with both hands, started tying it, one fold after another.

When he had finished, he looked at me again. Two tears spilled over from his eyes. They trickled down the creases in his cheeks leaving a trail of wetness, and disappeared into his beard.

Stone Games

Rizio Yohannan Raj

WE WERE IN THE MIDDLE of the second forenoon period when Sr. Agnes's strangely shaky voice reached us over the microphone to inform us that we had the afternoon off. That voice urged everyone to leave for home at the earliest. Ordinarily, our HM or headmistress's declaration of the day's independence would have been like manna from the heavens for us. But that was not how it was meant to be that day.

The nun's voice was bursting with emotion. It was a tragic moment; the country's prime minister had been shot by her own security guards.

At first, the odd sentiment in our rather solemn-voiced HM's announcement made us sneak a glance at one another in our typical pre-teen fashion, and giggle. The next instant something told us it was inappropriate behaviour, and we tried to focus on her words. I guess such timely appreciation of the context comes as a reward when a group of individuals develop a sense of community over time. While the import of what Sr. Agnes said did not quite sink in, despite our earnest attempt to be attentive, we heard one thing clearly: Everyone must get back home as fast as possible—do not spring up groups or join any gathering on the way.

As soon as the announcement ended, the school bell rang relentlessly for a minute to indicate it was the end of the day. Normally, the sound of it would have been the cue for us to grab our stuff and shoot ourselves out of the classroom, out of the arched school gate, and then out on to the street. But the very urgency in the HM's voice slowed us down; the rare emotion in it made us do exactly what it had urged us not to.

Instead of leaving as quickly as possible, we congregated in groups to linger, first on the verandahs, and then on the street corners, eavesdropping on the conversations of the older girls, teachers, shopkeepers, passersby... They all seemed to echo the same sentiment: No one was safe. No one could be trusted. As the event proved, not even the most powerful person in the land – the iron lady herself – was safe.

As we trudged back home, we did not talk to each other, but tried to take in everything happening around us. Like snakes in heat, we smelled the rising dust in town. We saw the big boys from the Government Boys High School gather at the junctions. We listened to their mounting voices forming dark clouds of sound over the intense streets.

We should have been playing marbles or seven stones through that afternoon. Light stone games. That is what we did as children during our leisure hours in the early eighties. To think of it, those games sort of trained us early enough to handle our dreams and desires as though they were flat stones or pebbles.

Consider the seize-throw game: People tend to believe that they can do wonderful things if they are let loose a little more than usual. From the safe zone of one's unadulterated imagination, everything looks easy and cool. That is how you end up watching a game of marbles from a distance, exclaiming: *Ah, why can't they do this simple thing of rolling the stones into those holes?* As a consequence of such a presumption, you long for an accidental day off, a sudden lottery win, the appearance of a genie… something to work the miracles you are destined to bring forth.

But outside these safe zones of the imagination, there is the bitter truth —you have never had the maturity to deal even with the smallest unanticipated freedom that has come your way. What a living hell it would be to be suddenly free from all the cares and structures within which you are securely trapped! If at all such a phantasmagoric sense of freedom descends, you would surely be at a loss as to what to do with its incredible offer of time and space. Fortuitous freedoms, however petty, are an intimation of your need for control—to control and to be controlled. They are a revelation of the conditional nature of your body and mind. When you land them, you are perplexed; you begin to drift, seize and throw things about, like stones.

Often, it takes a lifetime or more to gather your wits and find the right stones that might sink *the irrepressible,* which Kundera's title—*The Unbearable Lightness of Being*—has miraculously contained in a few words. But sometimes ripeness comes well in advance, and that too unexpectedly. And that is one of life's lessons that we learnt on 31 October 1984.

We did not play that afternoon. Not out of compulsion, but out of choice. We came back from school and, without even changing our clothes, assembled under the Jungle Jack tree in front of our house. That was our wont on holidays. But today we were not a set of kids at casual play; we were a reflective brood. None of us ventured to suggest any stone game to celebrate our chance freedom. The air was too petrified to evoke any longing for extra flint. Our mood offered no room for rambling either; we stuck to the big shade, like a heap of chips.

Yes, we got a day to ourselves. It was rare for convent schools like ours to get a working day free. No one considered us political or independent enough to be protesting on the streets for public causes. Of course, the senior girls got to go home early when the students from the government schools would come in a procession and explain the gravity of their protest to our headmistress. It is another matter that what convinced the holy sister to close the school was the threatening look on the faces of the boys rather than any identification with their cause. I am positive the girls and the teachers who got the benefit of those strikes hardly ever knew what the strikes were for. I doubt if they even cared!

By all means, the occasional downtime granted exclusively to the older students was unfair to the little ones in the primary section, and their teachers. I knew how it felt – we had been through it for six long years. Now, caught between the high-schoolers and the small kids, my upper primary class was not fully a part of the power structures of the world, though we were well on our way. It was in that neither-here-nor-there space of possibilities that the news of the guards' stones hit us.

Suddenly, we were filled with doubts about the notions of power and authority. Here was a situation that seemed to treat everyone on par. From tiny tots to tenth graders, everyone was asked to go home. Everyone was vulnerable, fearful, uncertain… No one was all too powerful or well-guarded against the dread on prowl. Everyone needed to reach a safe place. The day's breaking news was beginning to burst our perceptions of the hierarchical world and its severity. More breakages were to follow.

After three or four hours of returning home, we were still sitting under the Jungle Jack. It was way past lunchtime and our mothers seemed to have forgotten all about us. None of us ventured to get back home either. Of course, it was not unusual for our parents to let us be. Ours was a small-town neighbourhood of the early eighties. Children were not at all considered the primary reason for their parents' GAD*. We were supposed to mind our own business, while our parents went about their work. We did not live in walled colonies. We had the transcendental advantage of living in a largely seamless land—the clones of fences between compounds were ever too willing to fall off, and no one really cared. There prevailed a greater sense of belonging, trust and understanding. So, as children, no one stopped us from choosing our daily playgrounds between the extensive coconut groves or fields after the harvest, owned by different people whose names were simply navigational signs for us as we moved from one space to another.

To think back, we, including our subliminals, transgenders and itinerants, were quite a peaceful society, notwithstanding our daily arguments and passing jealousies. Irrespective of their creed, people took part in or contributed to all sorts of rituals and processions—whether in cash, kind, mind, muscle or spirit. The gods had not yet started their wars in our part of the world and our townspeople were yet to be recruited en masse as bonded labourers or guerrilla warriors towards the institution of particular divinities. Democracy prevailed in some way or the other, despite the fact that hardly anyone in our place had read or even seen a copy of the Constitution of India. Most middle-class folks from

---

*Generalised Anxiety Disorder

my generation first learnt about the National Emergency as a topic for school quizzes. The greatest agitations we saw during our school days were the strikes organised by the boys from the government high school to support or protest against something happening in other parts of the world. We did not know anything outside our own domestic concerns that could affect our play.

Most homes in our area did not yet have a television set—for some reason or the other, it was considered an enemy of school-going children. In any case, most of us did not think it worth our while to invest in a fight for a Dyanora TV set. My brother and I watched it in one of the homes in our neighbourhood and considered the design rather inelegant, even with the colour pictures. Besides, the programmes were mostly in English or Hindi. Growing up in a small Kerala town, we had no interest in letting these foreign languages affect our lives beyond the bearable school lessons and the delightful English and Hindi songs contained in the cassettes our uncles would bring home from Bombay and the faraway Gulf.

At home, we all had big Murphy or Philips radio sets that sat on elegant wooden stands. In my house, only Papa knew how to tune our Murphy, which entailed a grand exertion of fifteen to twenty minutes. The big radio sets were basically used on Saturday and Sunday afternoons for the afternoon news from Delhi, and practically no one except our fathers was interested in that. The rest of the family, to nurture its many-splendoured interests in music, cricket, football, boat racing, etc., pretended to forget internal differences and campaigned for transistor radios, cassette players and tape recorders. Some of them got lucky, while others harnessed their networking skills to access their voices of choice from the neighbourhood.

My parents were progressive and thought it was important for their children to listen to the daily news, some good music and radio plays. So we had our radio-cum-tape recorder at home. But that afternoon, the house was full of people—mostly my mother's friends from the locality. When we came home, they were all listening to the news updates, and talking loudly among themselves. We had no chance of laying any claims to the radio, when such a great adult interest was invested in it.

It is no wonder that all the neighbourhood women assembled in my house on such a day. My house had always been a haven for conversation by virtue of the social nature of my parents. It never surprised me to come back home and see a lot of adults gathered in our living room. And on this day, it was only natural that they hung out with our transistor radio and made a hell of a lot of noise, amidst which they even forgot that it was past lunchtime and their wards, back from school, were loafing. We, for our part, had no complaints; we understood it better than the adults that it was human nature to resist staying put when there was a call to be confined!

After an hour or so of staying together in stony silence under the Jungle Jack, the eldest among us, thirteen-year-old Reeja Peethambaran, known to us as Kochuvaava Chechi (the little-little older sister), went to her house and got a small transistor radio-cum-tape recorder. She was the only one of us who had direct access to such a device. In those days, most middle-class parents in our part of the world did not invest in a transistor-cum-cassette player, considering the backdrop of sibling rivalry and other prevailing in-house conflicts. The diverse interests of the members of the same household often forced the head of the household to decide against investing in such new-fangled gadgets. Consequently, someone who was an only child was more fortunate. Kochuvava Chechi was, in effect, a single child, since her elder brother was ten years older and a creature of the outdoors rather than interested in what was coming out of a radio.

We were all ears. For once the news hooked us, in the way music or sports commentaries normally would, beyond the barrier of language. We simply wanted to *know*—we did not care in which language. Before it was too late, we longed to be a part of the grave thing that had already gripped the nation. That was the first time I sat down to listen to a news bulletin. Otherwise, the only time I had ever heard the news was when the big radio was booming on Saturdays and Sundays, and I could not prevent the news from hitting my ears.

It took us some time to tune it to the Evening News. I can't recall what exactly we heard. But the newsreader certainly told us that the wait was over. Indira Gandhi was no more. The guards' stones had taken her life away.

We held each other's sweaty hands and listened, trying to make sense of the sentences. Beyond a quiz topic, Indira Gandhi had been nobody to us until that moment. But that afternoon, she became instrumental in making us conscious of a certain dynamic aspect of our selves which went far beyond our small static lives. For the first time, we became conscious of the processes of forming a collective, of sharing a sentiment, of feeling like a community. We were no longer a reckless playgroup. As we sat there, no one spoke, but everyone knew that for once, we wanted to discuss something larger than our own lives. But we did not know how to articulate that. Our headmistress's quivering words, *our Prime Minister has been shot...* were not mere words anymore. They came back to inform us that something drastic had happened to us as a people.

What was most intense for me was the realisation that the afternoon affected each one of us in some profound way. For once, we belonged to a universe much larger than home and school. What had happened demanded a response from us, and each one of us in our little company felt the weight of that responsibility. For once, we knew sharing happened beyond words. For once, we knew how the most significant things need not be communicated, but would be known to everyone concerned at the right time.

The strange thing was that, amidst all that sense of community, what I felt most acutely was an awareness of my own thought processes. It was a vague intimation, but I knew that beyond emotions, at a subjective level, my thoughts could be preoccupied with things that I did not yet know of. I wanted to use a different language to express this new consciousness of my own self. But I had no clue how to articulate it, how to give it the energy of an utterance. It was for the first time I was feeling the urge to speak about something outside of my own person. That afternoon starkly revealed to me that my world was a limited space; it looked for growth, connections and fulfillment in relationships with other worlds.

I listened to all the English news bulletins during the following days, which were declared holidays. I also read our Malayalam newspaper through and through, hungry for news and history. Different articles slowly started telling me of the Sikh demands for a separate state, of Operation Blue Star, of the circumstances that led to the assassination of Indira Gandhi, of the anti-Sikh riots bloodying North Indian streets…

I had never been to North India, and did not yet know even one Sikh. Yet, I felt the frustration of not being able to do anything about all that was happening around me, which was actually so far away. I had in a few days come to realise that the far can be so near and the near can be so far. It nearly killed me to think that I did not have a language that was adequate to communicate in such a situation. For the first time, I understood that it is nearly impossible to translate one's deepest thoughts and feelings, because it is not easy to exercise one's freedom of choice of words. Yet, the change that was possessing me helped me see that the women of my neighbourhood were not mere gossipmongers; they were individuals interested in the affairs of the world. I became convinced that mothers could legitimately think beyond their children's lunches. And, as a natural extension of all these awakenings, the elections of 1984 in December took up a lot of my interest, and the Christmas holidays were spent mostly in reading newspapers and periodicals, and following the local candidates.

It was a few years before I realised that those were indeed the days of my political initiation, that I was being reborn a political subject, that the home where I grew up was a space for political freedom. It was much later, when confronted by several stories of oppression and bondage, that I became truly grateful for my blessed childhood. Today, if I see the chain of events in India that have turned one political party from a tower of 404 seats in the eighth Lok Sabha into a veritable ruin in the sixteenth , while making it possible for another to go from a mere two seats to a near full house in the same three decades, it is thanks to 1984. The year was a message sent to me, inscribed on a stone tablet: There is a moment in everyone's life, where one clearly sees one's destiny in a life lived between silences and stone games.

It was amazing that in the same year, in the third term, we had to study the translation of an excerpt from *Letters from a Father to His Daughter* as part of our seventh-grade Malayalam course. It talked about the journey of a pebble from the moment of its break from the high mountains. It took us through the pebble's bumpy descent down the rocky slopes to the river followed by its drift through the waters for centuries before emerging as a sparkling pebble that shimmers without edges and moves on without bitterness to its ultimate destiny—which is to become a grain of sand with a world of experience.

I found it a deeply moving piece of writing. Maybe the fact that the assassination of the daughter, to whom it is addressed, was a ground-breaking event in my personal history of thought rendered the piece that much more poignant. It was indeed the first piece of writing that revealed to me that I was naturally inclined to contemplation. My brother and I were voracious readers, and our house had always been full of books and periodicals of various kinds. But never had a piece of writing so starkly intimated me of my organic affiliation with philosophy. Nehru's words to his daughter made me think of reading as an exercise towards a different level of understanding, a subtler appreciation of life that lay beyond grasping the concept, outside the delights offered by language. Paradoxically, they also made me see that I had to keep attempting to communicate the incommunicable, that I had to try and write myself out.

The following mid-summer vacation remains a landmark period in the history of my reading to this day. During those two months, I read almost all the major Malayalam fiction writers, at least their most famous works. I borrowed books from neighbours, exhausted the list of contemporary writers in the library and reading room in my mother's village, saved pocket money to buy books... That summer I came to learn one crucial thing about real writers, which I have since retained in my heart: Real writers never treat anyone below par, whether one is reading them as a naive eleven-year-old or getting to know them as an adult admirer.

Through the year following the assassination of Indira Gandhi, I read up a lot about the Emergency and the dark shadow it had cast on Indian democracy. It disturbed me to think that it was Jawaharlal's Priyadarshini who was the villain of those stories. It agitated me more, when I read what her son, the new prime minister of India, Rajiv Gandhi, said about the riots: 'When a big tree falls, the earth shakes.' I kept wondering what impression the story of the pebble had left on Jawaharlal's daughter and grandson. What and how did they lose it, why and where?

It was many years later in college that I read Malayalam writer NS Madhavan's short story, 'Van Marangal Veezhumpol' (When Big Trees Fall), which was written against the backdrop of the anti-Sikh riots. The story, set in a nuns' shelter run by the church, took me back to my convent days, specifically to the very day of my first political arousal – 31 October 1984. And I realised, when big trees fall, indeed the earth shakes, and the vibrations continue to fill our space. Maya Angelou was right when she wrote in her poem 'When Great Trees Fall': 'When great trees fall... / After a period, peace blooms.... / Spaces fill with a kind of soothing electric vibration... / We can be, be and be better...'

My political consciousness, triggered into being in October 1984, has since offered me many fascinating encounters beyond the world of literature. The most recent of these has been some of my poetic experiments inspired by artist Riyas Komu's work. In an attempt to understand the events that have scarred the country's history, in 2013, Riyas recovered nine *stone goddesses* from the ruins of independent India – The Partition Riots, Gandhi/Godse, 1969 Ahmedabad Riots, The Emergency, The Anti-Sikh Riots, Rath Yatra/Babri Masjid, Bombay Blasts, Poverty/Pokhran, and Godhra/Modi. I came across this nine-piece work two years later when I was interacting with the artist to bring his serial work, *International Worker's Day, Gandhi from Kochi,* to New Delhi. In the last week of October 2015, I was thinking of writing an article reflecting on the context of bringing this series of five Gandhi paintings by Riyas to Delhi. As part of my research for that, I looked at the way his Gandhi first appeared in Kochi—along with the nine stone goddesses. Suddenly it struck me that I was right on 31 October, the anniversary of one of the stone goddesses, which has just been renamed National Unity Day by the Indian government in the memory of Sardar Patel whose birth anniversary falls on the same day. The dramatic irony of that timing was too stark to escape my notice – National Unity Day falling on the day preceding the State Reorganisation Day!

As I got more involved with the date, it seemed to take the appearance of a stoned queen of drama in more ways than one. At about 9.20 a.m. on 31 October 1984, Indira Gandhi was on her way to be interviewed by British actor Peter Ustinov, who was filming a documentary for Irish television. She could not reach her interviewer; her assassins met her on her way and shot their stones right through her.

Within me, the profound effect of the drama of errors that seemed to surround India's iron lady even at the moment of her death in 1984 converged with the deadline of an Indo-Irish poetry project that I had been part of in 2015. Clearly, the last day of October was bringing me another stark awakening, more than three decades after it first touched me!

My memory of 1984 is quite clouded. Words and images from that year lie scattered in my head, like the spent afternoon sky of early autumn. Now, a mixed feeling rises against its horizon. Boundless, yet solid, like a mountain range. Somewhere, a stone cries. And it sounds like a series of poems raining.

Here is the prelude:

A Prelude to the Great Indian National Unity, from 31 October 1984

We have gone through much together, Dear Me,
and yet it suddenly occurs to me, we don't know each other at all.

Peter Ustinov in his autobiography *Dear Me*

Peter Ustinov,
did it disappoint you
that she chose death over you?

In India, where death is a demonic god,
we say guests are as good as gods.
Our premier had to attend to you, at any cost,

but, to think of it, that day,
were you her guest,
or was she your guest?

Between your Irish television and her Indian office
you were to host her, and she was to host you—
bizarre, but that mix-up always happens

at the cusp of a promise and its fulfillment—
you lose sense of causes and reasons,
you get lost between your roles

as a witness and an accomplice. It is hard
to understand such moments of crossing,
but now you might be able to look

an unfulfilled promise in its very human eye,
and perhaps forgive all iron-willed ones, since
you too have known the molten taste of death—

Nothing remains in its rock solid state of unity, Peter,
we know, for we have endured many conversions
of a Mahatma within us—we have seen his ethical fibre

turn into a splintered emotion, his vital element lock
itself inside our continuing struggle for independence,
his statues desperately stand for our crumbling dreams.

Peter, had you observed the six seasons of India,
you would have got wind of the shifting of time,
of the hour becoming ripe for the fall of the fruit.

That you were caught unawares, were still waiting
for your bud of inspiration at the hour of bereavement,

contains a warning for our today, which is your future:

actors must surrender to nature and
gather their signs like wild children do, for
intimations come as stones, flowers and twigs.

You had an astounding Irish clue, Peter,
it was Halloween—the twilight hour that shuttles
one between the dead and the living;

a day that gives one the magnificently playful hope
that one's children can scare one's ghosts away—
a faith strangely rooted in and belonging to one's dread.

Terror has come to sit in the heart of our affairs,
and the strange futures of our centuries' old faiths
have now become so intertwined with our fears.

Ustinov, Peter Ustinov, like you,
after having gone through much together,
and trying to stay united in our transits,

Dear us, Dear us, Dear us,
we too have come to a sudden realisation:
we do not recognise ourselves at all,

on this great day of national unity,
this hell of a halloween time, as we try
to scare our ghosts away, our masks blind us.

Does our bewilderment relieve you
of your disillusionment about India's Priyadarshini
choosing death in the garden over you?

New Delhi (31 Oct–6 Dec 2015)

A House of Lies

Hartosh Singh Bal

ON 1 NOVEMBER 1984, THE journalist Sanjay Suri, who was reporting on the violence unfolding against the Sikhs in Delhi in the aftermath of Indira Gandhi's assassination, went to Gurudwara Rakab Ganj near the Parliament House in Delhi after hearing of a mob gathered outside. He wrote at the time:

> On the evening of November 1, I went to Gurudwara Rakab Ganj at about 4 p.m. on hearing of trouble there. I was assigned to go there because I am a staff reporter with *The Indian Express*. I had been there for a short while when I saw Mr. Gautam Kaul, then Additional Commissioner of Police of New Delhi range, standing to a side.
>
> Outside the Gurudwara I saw a crowd of about 4,000 men led by Congress-I leader Kamal Nath. At the time I went there, the crowd was on the road. Some were making weak attempts to enter the Gurudwara, but the Congress I MP and other leaders of the same party who were with him were keeping them under some control.
>
> I learnt that earlier in the day there had not been

> such control, and that the mob had tried to enter the Gurudwara. They retracted when some men fired from within the Gurudwara. After that at least two Sikhs outside the Gurudwara were lynched by the mob. When I reached there I saw the bodies of two men, both Sikhs, still burning on the roadside. There were rumours that four non-Sikhs had been burnt inside the Gurudwara, but the police said they had entered the Gurudwara, searched every place but found no hostages or bodies.
>
> As is evident from television shots that day, Mr. Gautam Kaul was conducting mourners at Teen Murti house when firing, killing and burning was taking place close by in the area under his charge. When he did come, he stood to a side without making any efforts to check the crowd. Leaders of the crowd seemed fully in charge. At one point a group charged towards the Gurudwara gate to a side near which Mr. Kaul stood. But seeing them he retreated instead of checking them. The police officer was obviously a passive spectator to commands by Congress-I leaders. (From the affidavit submitted to the Misra Commission)

Three decades later Sanjay Suri was to write:

> Did I see Kamal Nath physically and obviously leading a mob, commanding them to kill Sikhs? No, I did not. If to that extent the affidavit (filed before the Ranganath Misra commission set up in 1985 to probe the violence) was 'weak', so it was and so be it. But it is just as true that what I had seen raised disturbing questions about just what Kamal Nath was doing there. These were questions the commissions of inquiry did not probe at any length.

> What I did see then was that when the crowd surged forward at one point, Kamal Nath had only to gesture lightly, and they held back. Does that fact exonerate Kamal Nath? Because, on the face of it, he had restrained the crowd, hadn't he? By way of some intervention, he did at that point prevent the crowd advancing further towards the Gurudwara.
>
> Why did the crowd listen to him? Why, in a situation where a murderous bunch was advancing yet again, would the police continue to stand to a side (and the officer leading them duck to a side), and now watch the MP control that crowd? Why did a word from the Congress MP become more effective than any move from the police? What was the relation between Kamal Nath and that crowd that he had only to raise his hand towards it and it held back?

Two Sikhs were lynched, and then, dead or alive, they were set on fire, their bodies burning as a senior leader of the Congress stood by at the head of a mob, and the police led by Additional Commissioner Gautam Kaul, a cousin of Rajiv Gandhi, watched. Two Sikhs among the thousands killed in Delhi over three days does not sound like much, but the killings took place within a kilometre of the Indian Parliament. It was the one incident of communal killings where a senior Congress leader was present at the head of a murderous mob composed of Congress loyalists. It was also an illustration of how the police, led by the senior-most Delhi policeman to be on the streets that day, did nothing to intervene.

Two days later, on 3 November, *The Statesman* reported, 'Policemen criticised the role of politicians too. Several councillors, they alleged, interceded on behalf of violent mobs when policemen tried to stop arson. Officers wondered what Mr. Kamal Nath was doing at Rakab Ganj.' Besides non-imposition of curfew, there was criticism of the lack of crisp commands from the top; '"Senior officers only asked what was wrong over the wireless without once suggesting what could be done," one officer said.'

That is it. From that point on, the role of Kamal Nath and Gautam Kaul, as well as the fate of the two murdered Sikhs disappeared from public memory to be invoked only when a commission of inquiry released a report, or when a debate over the role of Narendra Modi in 2002 had to be derailed.

Kamal Nath escaped because from the very beginning the demand for justice for the victims of the 1984 violence never got the media attention it deserved. I have always felt this lack of media attention was tied to the events in Punjab that followed the massacres in Delhi. As terrorist violence spiralled, to speak of this demand was to echo the grievances that many terror groups in Punjab were echoing to justify their own violence. It is, to use the terminology in fashion in India today, as if the very demand for justice had become anti-national.

I chose to follow the coverage of the national newsmagazine *India Today*, at the time by far the most influential news publication in the country, through much of this period to see if my conjecture had any truth to it.

In 1984, the magazine was a fortnightly, and the dating follows a technical procedure. The 30 November 1984 issue that covered the massacres of the Sikhs over the first week of November would have been available on 15 November. That would be true of all subsequent issues of the magazine mentioned in this essay.

In that issue, the magazine reported in an article entitled 'The Violent Aftermath':

> The carnage that swept so much of the national capital and parts of the country last fortnight was an unprecedented, uniform reaction to the slaying of Prime Minister Indira Gandhi by two of her own guards.
>
> The pattern, most vivid and bloody in Delhi, was nauseatingly repeated elsewhere: spontaneous arson and destruction at first taken over by criminally led hoodlums who killed Sikhs, looted or burnt their homes and properties while the police twiddled their thumbs.
>
> In some places, the Sikhs responded with counter violence, inviting harsher retribution, but the casualties spanned both communities. Several hospitals reported that casualties coming to them were a mixture of Sikhs and Hindus. But the Sikhs were outnumbered, and soon it became an unequal battle.
>
> In retrospect, there is general agreement that the army should have been called out the first day, if only as a precautionary measure. The army was called out in the early afternoon of November 1, but was nowhere in sight that day. Isolated lorries began to be seen that night, and the next day the army presence was more evident.
>
> But nothing short of a judicial inquiry can show why the army clampdown was not fully to effect till after the cremation on November 3. But it is known that while Rajiv Gandhi was keen to call in the army on the first evening itself, he was advised by Home Minister Narasimha Rao to wait a while.

> Gross though their failure was, the culpability of the police in the tragedy would rank next only to that of the Congress(I) politicians in Delhi.
>
> At over two dozen scenes of violence that *India Today* correspondents visited in the course of their investigations, the local people, including Hindus, pointed the finger at the local Congress(I) leaders.

From the very beginning, the coverage introduced elements that were to bedevil all subsequent inquiries into the violence.

The report speaks of 'spontaneous arson and destruction at first taken over by criminally led hoodlums who killed Sikhs'. This has remained the dominant narrative. So much so that today, more than thirty years later, President Pranab Mukherjee in his memoirs has chosen to blame 'hoodlums' for the '84 violence. The possibility that the Congress as an institution organised the violence was never even up for scrutiny.

Two other points are of great importance. The report, despite not having a byline, authoritatively states, 'But it is known that while Rajiv Gandhi was keen to call in the army on the first evening itself, he was advised by Home Minister Narasimha Rao to wait a while.' Even today, it is not clear what the source for this authoritative assertion is, and no facts have emerged to support it. This hurry to absolve Rajiv Gandhi and his family of any direct involvement, and shield the prime minister from accountability for the violence that unfolded during his watch has also been part of an ongoing narrative.

Finally, and this is in keeping with the tendency to absolve the party high command of any responsibility for the violence, the report observed, '...local people, including Hindus, pointed the finger at the local Congress(I) leaders'. But this does nothing to explain the coordinated nature of violence across the city, from the slogans to the use of tyres and kerosene to incinerate the living.

In its 15 December 1984 issue, *India Today* ran the following article entitled 'Riot victims: Unending Nightmare'. In that article it said:

> As the slayings on November 1 and 2 shook the capital, Sikh families in the affected areas had fled often with only the clothes on their backs to the nearest refuge they could find. Spurred by fear of the mobs, they invaded police stations, government buildings (primarily schools) and gurudwaras. According to estimates, about 50,000 of them had to flee their homes.
>
> Up against a situation it had never faced before, the local administration didn't seem to know initially quite what to do: the numbers seemed unmanageable. The Government finally declared 10 places as officially recognised camps.
>
> In actual terms, however, the displaced were scattered in dozens of sites across the length and breadth of Delhi. The biggest single camp was in Shahdara, where the number was estimated at well over 10,000. But if the murders and arson showed the ugly face of Delhi, in the aftermath of the violence there seemed some signs of hope. Professionals and government employees, businessmen and children, college students and traders and housewives, joined hands to supplement the Government effort that was the butt of much criticism.
>
> But the odds were clearly heavy. On November 11, not even 10 days after the mayhem had died down, the relief camps started closing down one by one.

> The scenario turned even more frightening as allegations of the involvement of local Congress(I) leaders started pouring in, not only in Delhi but also from other affected northern Indian states.
>
> The allegations were concretised in a report titled 'Who are the guilty?' which was drafted jointly by the People's Union for Democratic Rights (PUDR) and People's Union for Civil Liberties (PUCL) ... (The report) was made public on November 15 ...
>
> While Prime Minister and Congress(I) President Rajiv Gandhi is reported to have asked for a probe by party leaders into the allegations, nothing very much seems to have come of it since.

Again, as the evidence against individual Congressmen continued to mount, it became clear the government was not interested in the plight of the victims. Relief camps were closed down within ten to fifteen days of the violence with no proper facilities for rehabilitation in place. Many had to return to localities where the murderers of their families roamed free.

Once again, without any sourcing, the magazine indicated 'that Prime Minister and Congress(I) President Rajiv Gandhi is reported to have asked for a probe by party leaders into the allegations' only to conclude 'nothing very much seems to have come of it since'. It is difficult to believe that any journalist or news organisation can make such a claim without taking it further. How is it possible that no probe ever took place if the party president had asked for it? The tendency to absolve Rajiv Gandhi of any direct responsibility, evident in the reportage of the violence, emerges again.

In its following issue, 31 December 1984, *India Today* published an article related to the national election that took place towards the end of 1984. It is entitled 'Poll publicity: Medium is the massage'. There it wrote:

> Even in the print media, the appeal is to the emotions. Fear: Will the country's border finally be moved to your doorstep? Suspicion: Why should you feel uncomfortable riding in a taxi driven by a taxi-driver who belongs to another state?
>
> Dread: Will your groceries list in the future include acid bulbs, iron rods, daggers? The visual images lend support: barbed wire, crocodiles, cacti, knives. But there's deliverance too: Your vote can stop your groceries list turning into an arms inventory...Your vote for the Congress(I).

In another report entitled 'Congress(I): Great expectations' that appeared in the same issue, it was said:

> The forecast shows that the Congress(I)'s main message, that the unity and integrity of the country are threatened, has effectively gone home. It is a message that seems to have evoked a compelling response: some 47 per cent of the electorate believes that the most important issue in the election was the unity of the country while 30 per cent talked of inflation and 18 per cent of corruption.

These two reports appeared just before the national election that took place less than two months after the November massacre. The description of the Congress advertising campaign is chilling. It was clearly designed to evoke a communal threat, with the Sikhs cast as villains. But the reportage betrays no admission of this fact, talking only of the evocation of fear in the abstract. In light of this campaign, the positive spin to the results, seeing it as a mandate on the threat to the unity of the country, betrays a cynicism, a disregard for the cost of this victory.

In *India Today's* 15 February 1985 issue, Aroon Purie and TN Ninan interviewed Prime Minister Rajiv Gandhi. That interview was published in an article entitled 'People's expectations are scary'. An excerpt that pertains to the anti-Sikh pogrom that took place less than four months ago appears below:

Q. Besides the political demands, there still seems to be a certain sense of insecurity amongst the Sikhs.
A. We have done a lot. The major insecurity was in Delhi after the beginning of November. Most of the people who left have started coming back. People from Alwar have started coming back, some people from Punjab have started coming back. We have taken steps for their protection and rehabilitation in Delhi.

Q. What about the judicial inquiry?
A. We don't think it will help at the moment. It would raise issues which are really dead.

Q. How do you react to Bhajan Lal's proposal to merge Punjab, Haryana, and Himachal Pradesh?
A. It is a huge question and I do not think we have discussed it enough to just react to it. No. I don't object to it. It is something we could look into provided it does satisfy the people in Punjab. They are part of the solution, we cannot push something like this on them.

This is the first interview that Rajiv Gandhi gave after becoming prime minister. The interview was conducted by Aroon Purie, the owner of the magazine, and TN Ninan, who even today remains one of our best-known editors. The fate of the victims of the '84 violence comes up, but the answer, 'We have taken steps for their protection and rehabilitation in Delhi', escapes scrutiny; we get no idea of what the government has really done for them. The next answer is frightening, and it comes from the prime minister of the country: 'We don't think it will help at the moment. It would raise issues which are really dead.' Why does he think a judicial probe into the violence will not help? Why does he consider the issues dead? The interviewers don't seem to have thought of asking evident follow-up questions. We are mere months away from the violence. No one has been held culpable. There has been no movement towards justice. Yet, two of our most eminent media personalities let the prime minister get away with lies!

As for how dead the issues of justice were, this becomes evident from a report filed in the same issue of the magazine. It is entitled 'First suit filed on behalf of Sikh victims of post Mrs Gandhi assassination violence':

> Life had been going rather well for 37-year-old Shivcharan Singh. Part-owner of a printing press in Bombay, he often travelled to Delhi to be with his wife Harpreet Kaur, daughter Vimi, 7, and son Vikky, 4.
>
> When not busy at the press, he helped an amateur theatrical group stage plays. So it was to be just another trip to Delhi when the expectant Shivcharan boarded the Janata Express in Bombay on October 31 with a dozen colleagues from a theatre group.
>
> The theatre group made it to Delhi, but Vimi and Vikky never saw their father again. Shivcharan's journey came to a

> fiery end beside the track at the Tughlakabad railway station near Delhi where he was dragged out of the sleeper coach by a bloodthirsty mob, beaten senseless and then set on fire while still half-alive.
>
> Soon he was just another number on the list of 2,717 Sikhs killed in Delhi and elsewhere following Mrs Gandhi's assassination.
>
> But Harpreet Kaur was not willing to write off her husband as just another statistic. She and her children have started legal proceedings seeking Rs 6 lakh in damages and compensation from the Government for the inability of its employees to protect Shivcharan from the mob at Tughlakabad station.
>
> Her lawyers, K.T.S. Tulsi and D.S. Narula, have served notice on the home secretary, the Lt. Governor of Delhi and the general manager of the Northern Railway to pay the damages or face a suit in the high court. This is the first suit filed on behalf of Sikh victims of the post assassination violence by lawyers Tulsi and Narula. Several more now are under preparation.

Even as Rajiv Gandhi claimed that the quest for justice for the victims of the '84 violence involved issues that were now dead, the situation in Punjab continued to worsen. Among the most potent issues driving the violence and terror in Punjab was the fate of the victims of the '84 violence.

In its 15 April 1985 issue, in an article titled 'Punjab: Moving cautiously', *India Today* wrote, 'Like the Bhindranwale tapes of yore, video cassettes, and tape-recorded statements of Delhi riot victims are being freely hawked in and around the Golden Temple. The SGPC added its bit to this last fortnight by releasing for free distribution a booklet in Punjabi recounting the atrocities in graphic, gory detail.'

The tone of this observation is perhaps the most telling comment on why the process of justice for the dead of '84 never got the attention it deserved, not just from the government but from the media. The copy seems to suggest that to speak of the unaddressed atrocities that took place in Delhi was on par with the divisive speeches of a Bhindranwale. It was as if, long before the BJP made the phrase fashionable, speaking or disseminating material about the 3,000 deaths in Delhi was itself an anti-national act.

In the issue that followed, the 30 April 1985 issue, there was a report on what was going on in Punjab in an article entitled 'Punjab: A Turning Point':

> Cassandras were out in force last fortnight in Amritsar as tension rose like mercury. With the Akalis set to resume their agitation from the Golden Temple and the Government firm on holding a national integration meeting in the adjoining Jallianwala Bagh as part of its "peace offensive" it was going to be another landmark Baisakhi.
>
> A landmark it certainly was but of a vastly different kind, not the cataclysm that was feared but a welcome turning point in the fortuitous Punjab saga. For once, Baisakhi was truly what it should be, the beginning of a new season of hope.
>
> Even as 50 companies of the Central Reserve Police Force (CRPF) and Border Security Force (BSF) fanned along the common approaches to the Golden Temple and Jallianwala Bagh and people waited tensely for the moment of reckoning, the news from Delhi came rattling

> over the teleprinters, drowning the din of contention with its forceful message.
>
> In a flash, the Centre announced it had ordered a probe by a sitting Supreme Court judge into the riots in Delhi following Mrs Gandhi's assassination, lifted the ban on the All India Sikh Students Federation (AISSF) which provided Bhindranwale many of his key storm troopers and all his gun-fodder, and gave broad hints of release of more Akali and AISSF leaders. In one stroke the most relevant of demands of the Sikhs had been conceded.

Finally the probe into the '84 violence was to become a reality, five months after the violence. In contrast, the inquiries into the communal violence in Bombay in 1992 and Gujarat in 2002 were announced within days of the end of the violence. In this case, the probe was not the act of a government that felt justice needed to be done. Instead, it was an act of negotiation with the Sikh leadership in the anticipation of some negotiated settlement to the violence in Punjab. Rajiv Gandhi had already declared the quest for justice was dead. Now he was reviving it purely as an instrumental goal. The media seems to have bought into the charade. For *India Today,* a probe into the massacre of 3000 Indian citizens in Delhi was not something necessitated in any civilised state. Rather it was a concession made to fulfill one of the relevant 'demands of the Sikhs'.

In the months to follow, the Supreme Court judge appointed to the probe, Ranganath Misra, was to violate every due procedure that was necessary in such an inquiry. The names of the victims were made public, the names of the perpetrators were closely guarded. The victims had to testify in the open, subject to cross-examination, while officials testified behind closed doors with lawyers appearing for the victims not allowed to hear them, leave alone cross-examine them. Victims were intimidated, Misra's role took on a partisan hue. The media, illegally, was barred from covering the proceedings. Unsurprisingly, right through the next year as the probe was on, *India Today* did not see it fit to carry a single story on what was going on.

For his untiring efforts, Ranganath Misra was subsequently made the chairman of the National Human Rights Commission and then given a seat in the Rajya Sabha by the Congress.

A Question of Identity

Preeti Gill

WHEN I LOOK BACK ON 31 October 1984, the first thing I recall with stark intensity is the silence of the street below my office in Delhi's Connaught Place. The sort of silence you associate with desolate, empty landscapes stretching vast and endless as far as the eye can traverse. Certainly not what you would expect the very heart of a throbbing metropolis, which is also the capital of the country, to look like in the middle of the day. But as I descended from the first floor of my office building with a friend, it was just such a scene of quiet emptiness that greeted me and it seemed to bring into the gentle autumn air a chill, a foretaste of something terrible that was waiting in the wings to fly in and claim me. And I am not a fanciful person given to a vivid imagination.

Indira Gandhi, India's prime minister and one of the most powerful, wily and shrewd politicians, had been shot by her Sikh (that they were both Sikhs was discovered later) bodyguards as she was leaving her house on Akbar Road, in what is called Lutyens' Delhi, to walk to her office in the adjoining bungalow. All the information that we'd been given before we were asked to leave the office as soon as possible for the safety of our homes was that she was in the All India Institute of Medical sciences (AIIMS)—India's premier medical facility at the time where all VIPs were treated. There was no 24x7 television coverage of news and events then and all we had to rely on for news was the State-owned TV channel, Doordarshan, which came on air every evening for a few hours and the State-controlled radio of course, which was strangely silent, muffled perhaps by the State apparatus. The news that Mrs Gandhi had succumbed to her injuries was out by about 1 p.m. and the special afternoon editions of some dailies reported it.

We were told that there were crowds of people swarming the streets around AIIMS. That senior politicians and officials were rushing there anxious about what this would mean. And perhaps at that very point when it was announced that she had died, rioting broke out in the seething mass of humanity that cluttered one of Delhi's major arterial roads. Armed with sticks and burning torches, a mob of about twenty men pounced on the cavalcade of the President of India, Giani Zail Singh who was a Sikh himself, when he was heading to AIIMS to see the body of the assassinated prime minister. I was to read this later for it was widely reported in the next morning's newspapers. Luckily, his limousine drove past without a scratch but the car that his press secretary was travelling in was damaged. Was it this incident that marked the beginning of the terrible bloodletting that was soon unleashed on the Sikhs, a small minority who had thus far been regarded as the protectors of their Hindu brothers, two sides of the same coin? The killings left almost 3000 innocent people dead in the capital city, savaged in the most brutal way. Over the next few days, Doordarshan continued to broadcast the most disturbing footage of the prime minister's body lying in state, then being taken for cremation, then lying on the funeral pyre, and all this while her agitated countrymen screamed bloodthirsty slogans like 'khoon ka badla khoon se lenge'. Somehow no one was quite prepared for what was later proved to be orchestrated murder and mayhem that split communities and shattered the peace of many of India's major cities.

Growing up in Central India, in the state of Madhya Pradesh, I had never really thought of myself as a Sikh. My family name, of course, established me as one. With a father who was a non-practicing Sikh, an agnostic actually, and a mother, an Arya Samaji who came from Abbottabad, now in Pakistan, my siblings and I had a very sketchy notion of who we were (or at least of our religion) in a country where caste and religious denomination defines your identity even more than class and gender. This was possibly very aberrant behaviour on the part of my parents, or at the very least, it was way ahead of the times.

Like so many Hindu Punjabi and Sikh families who had made the long tortuous trek to India in the wake of Independence, my mother's family had arrived in this newly minted country on one of the last trains from Pakistan. Finding shelter in a tiny house in crowded Daryaganj in Old Delhi, my grandparents and their numerous offspring crowded into their very first ashiana or nest in their new homeland. It is a familiar story that echoes those told by many Partition survivors, but it is the story we inherited – of a family of refugees who had been part of the kafilas criss-crossing the arid plains of North India, who had seen blood, death, hunger and deprivation and struggled against huge odds before making good. These were the stories handed down by my grandparents in a sprawling house in Jabalpur, which was aptly named Ashiana. To be confronted with images of screaming mobs baying for blood was not something that seemed within the realm of possibility. Rather it belonged to the Partition narrative of my grandparents' generation.

That evening, despite the kind of rumours making the rounds and the extremely hysterical and rabblerousing images on TV, my husband—a clean-shaven Sikh—and I left our house in Bapa Nagar to attend a dinner party at the home of a friend in faraway Greater Kailash. (My parents had just left for Chandigarh; my father had gone on deputation and was allowed to retain his house in Bapa Nagar, which is where we were staying along with my sister.) We did not expect trouble. This was our city, our country after all. What happened on our return journey, however, belied our expectations.

It happened while driving down Delhi's Ring Road, somewhere near the busy Lajpat Nagar area and just before climbing the Lajpat Nagar flyover. That flyover is one of the oldest flyovers in the city. We had often sat there on balmy summer evenings, with ice-cream cones in hand, watching the traffic go by. That night, we suddenly ran into a crowd of men holding flaming torches, lathis, barchchas and the like. They seemed to emerge out of the dark, fearful and dangerous in their intensity. Just half an hour before this, we had been warned over the telephone by my sister, who had stayed home that night, that the television was full of disturbing news, that there was trouble brewing, and that we should return right away and be careful on our return journey. Those men forced my husband, who was driving, to stop the car. They roughly pulled open the doors on either side and leaned in, yelling, 'Sardar hai?'(Is there a Sardar/Sikh inside?) 'No,' we shouted back, fear making us nervous. In that instant my husband and I both wondered what answer we'd give if they asked our names. Chances are, we would have come up with safe-sounding Hindu names – Gupta, Aggarwal, Sharma... only his name and mine would have been different. Luckily, they did not ask. Neither for our names nor for his driving licence. They let us drive away because they thought we were Hindu like them. The fact that my husband did not wear a turban actually saved his life. He revealed to me later that he saw what looked like human figures being torched on the road below the flyover but I am immeasurably relieved that he did not point that out to me that evening. The incident left us all shaken, even traumatised. Over the years, it has sat somewhere in the furthest recesses of my mind, afraid to come to the fore because it contains within it so many questions and much rethinking of our universe.

It was just one small incident, and not a particularly terrible one compared to the many others that overtook a whole section of Indians, destroying lives, homes, livelihoods, faith, trust, friendship, relationships...What incidents like this brought home to me, and to many others like me who are educated, upper middle-class, apolitical and irreligious, is that identity is a huge marker. Your name spells out who you are, the community or religion in which you are born, which then pins you to a spot where you remain fixed and unmoving, under a spotlight, waiting to be accepted and feted or rejected and marginalised. Whether we define ourselves in that way is immaterial. It is who we are seen to be that matters enormously. Identification affects experience. It is the most mundane thing and yet it matters in the most significant, extraordinary way in our everyday lives.

Richard Jenkins says in *Social Identity* that we must first decide what we mean by 'identity'. It is knowing who we are, knowing who others are, them knowing who we are, us knowing who they think we are and so on. I, who had always thought of myself as an individual with my own responses, opinions and ideas and not part of any group, had suddenly been forced to accept this Sikh identity. I had become the hated Other who was responsible for the murder of the nation's mother; the one who must wear the crown of thorns for the great betrayal of trust where her Sikh bodyguards conspired to pump bullets into her body.

I, therefore, regard 1984 and what happened in the three days following the assassination of the prime minister as a traumatic moment in the history of our nation. A moment that witnessed the birth of a minority and tore communities apart, in somewhat the same way as Partition had done. The hatred and bloodletting that engulfed the nation in those three days of November 1984 left close to 3000 Sikhs dead in Delhi alone and some 50,000 were people forced to take shelter in relief camps, because their homes had been destroyed. It is apparent that this would have far-reaching consequences, that things would never be the same. I wonder whether the Sikh community has even now come to grips with the fact of the 1984 killings and how totally unexpected, horrific and intense they were. And it is so much worse because it is a period that has not been talked about enough, not debated enough; the wounds have been plastered over and they still reveal themselves as raw and bleeding each time someone brings up this subject and calls it the Sikh riots. The Sikhs did not riot; they were massacred.

Much like me, many Sikhs draw parallels between 1984 and what happened during the bloody partition of the subcontinent in 1947. I recall reading somewhere an interview with a survivor, who lost all his sons in 1984, making this very point. His anguish was uncontrollable because he had escaped unharmed along with his entire family when they fled from Lahore in 1947 and now in 'free India', where they should have been safe, his family had been destroyed. The past, therefore, in many ways, has been recast in the minds of the survivors, and indeed all those who were witness to the carnage of 1984. Many of the rumours that floated and became gospel in those days were about water tanks being poisoned, about houses being marked, about mobs of rioters being paid to do their pillaging and killing. It was such a time of fear and dread that one did not quite know what to believe. However, the one thing that is clear is that a very visible, very dominant community of prosperous farmers, landlords, shopkeepers, businessmen, soldiers and policemen was transformed into a minority overnight through concentrated violence and brutality. The realisation of their minority status was brought home to the Sikhs in many ways, including being told repeatedly that they formed a miniscule two percent of the country's population and as such were entitled to just that much by way of jobs and quotas.

Personally for me this minority status revealed itself in strange ways and there are two instances that I wish to cite here. We left Delhi in 1985 for a two-year stint in Nagpur where my husband's company had posted him. On our return to Delhi in May 1987, we stayed with my sister while we searched for a flat to rent. That proved to be an impossible task. People who met us liked us but became suspicious and hesitant to rent their properties to us as soon as they found out that we were Sikhs. It was as though we had grown horns or claws to become some sort of strange animals who could not be allowed into their houses. It was the shaping of a minority consciousness and it came as a shock for me for I'd studied in Delhi and lived there for years, and now it was as if I had been transformed into an alien outsider. The bitterness and anger that this caused stayed with us and when we went searching for a school for our six-year-old daughter we turned towards a 'minority' institution, Guru Harkishan Public School. I don't quite know why we did this. Was it the need to stick to 'our own people'? Was it a desire to inculcate in our child the principles of Sikhism in which I had not been educated? Or was it just that we knew that this school would welcome our child and not turn us away because we were Sikh? It is another matter that we decided to take her out of there within a year because she was already picking up on the community's anger, suspicion and bitterness, which was not something we wanted to burden her with. It seemed like a new language had been coined that was ugly and threatening, and it reflected how these children had already internalised the communal feelings of their parents and other adults. So many friends talked to us about the daily taunts, humiliations and indignities that they faced when they went to work, of young men blowing smoke in their faces, of being accosted by strangers, of having to explain themselves and their beliefs. So many decided to leave Delhi and make their lives in Punjab. We escaped all of this because of our non-Sikh appearance.

The sense of insecurity faced by the community was compounded by the fact that it felt abandoned by the State. It had withdrawn its protection. It had described the killings as natural and inevitable; it had also refused to call the guilty to book, to punish the killers. Instead, they had been rewarded with plum posts and fancy titles. Many years later, my daughter, while studying history at JNU, made up her mind to do her dissertation on 1984. She had heard us talk about 'those days' at home and decided that she wanted to see for herself what had happened to the victims and talk to the survivors. As she went to the resettlement colonies and hunted out people to interview, she became silent and withdrawn. I opened the door to her room one afternoon to find her listening to her tape recorder, the earphones plugged into her ears and tears rolling silently down her cheeks. She was weeping in helpless anger, sitting there by herself and dealing with the hurt and trauma of an entire community. It is a moment I remember with sharp pain. It was as if she, too, had taken on the garb of potential victimhood.

What she said to me when I brought this up much later is also something that has stayed with me. She said, 'I was introduced to 1984 as an *event* and I now feel it is an integral part of me. I may not have lived through it, but I too remember.'

Five months before the November 1984 carnage, the sacred Golden Temple was desecrated in a pitched battle fought inside its precincts in an anti-insurgency operation that became known as Operation Blue Star. Those two events led many to understand, for the first time, what another, larger minority had always felt like and they developed a new sensitivity to the insecurity that is part and parcel of being Muslim in a largely Hindu India. Even people who were relatively well off and in prominent positions of power felt that they had become vulnerable to mob violence and could no longer count on police protection. It was difficult for them to communicate their sense of hurt and resentment at this sudden turnabout even to their closest friends, many of whom had started to avoid them. That is something I heard from my parents later and it stunned me. Is it that easy to jettison the familiarity and trust of long years of association and friendship?

There are some well-known stories told by prominent people of what happened once news of Mrs Gandhi's assassination spread and the one that I am struck by was written by Amitav Ghosh who was teaching in Delhi University at the time and who happened to be on a bus passing by AIIMS on that day. There are two things that stand out for me in that story, which was published in *The New Yorker* in 1995. They concern what happened when a Sikh, who had boarded the bus at Connaught Place, was forced to hide from menacing bands of young men gathered around AIIMS. First is the sentence: 'He was a Sikh, but I (Ghosh) scarcely noticed this at the time,' and then: 'A stout woman in a sari sitting across the aisle from me was the first to understand what was going on. Rising to her feet, she gestured urgently at the Sikh, who was sitting hunched in his seat. She hissed at him in Hindi, telling him to get down and keep out of sight.' The reaction of the bus driver and the co-passengers in the bus to protect a Sikh, a man unknown to them, was instinctive. Then what happened to change all this within a few hours?

There were many Sikhs in the crowds milling around AIIMS on that fateful day. We know that now through newspaper reports and statements made before inquiry commissions. They felt confident, safe. Moreover, they, too, were there to mourn the death of their prime minister but within a few short hours everything changed. The behaviour of the crowd turned ugly and suddenly fearful, and the Sikhs started melting away. The security forces and the police deployed in huge numbers were everywhere and yet they remained mute spectators when the attacks began. This failure of the State machinery, their callous disregard of their duty to protect the life and property of citizens is what is most unforgivable. They could have contained the violence, stopped the killings, the arson and the looting but they did not. They turned away; they actively abetted the killings in some instances like the horrible massacre in Block 32 of Trilokpuri where 400 Sikhs were killed, or they stayed silent while the Sikhs were, quite literally, being burnt to death.

A journalist friend, who covered the anti-Sikh riots for a foreign newspaper, told me much later that he'd been there and he had heard the screaming silence of these murders. What made it even worse for him was the fact that these were rickshaw pullers, autowallahs, mechanics living out their lower middle-class lives. He remembers going to the railway station and seeing the bodies in the coaches and being reminded of Khushwant Singh's powerful images from *Train to Pakistan*. Rajiv Gandhi, the son of the slain prime minister and her successor, seemed to justify the mob violence and explain it away as a natural corollary of the assassination. He likened the carnage to the earth shaking when a mighty tree is uprooted ('When a big tree falls, it is only natural that the earth around it shakes a little'). The statement made at a rally he addressed at the Boat Club on 19 November 1984 created a sensation. It inflamed the families of those thousands of innocent citizens of this country who had been massacred, and also set the tone for the cover-up to come in the years that followed when, despite two judicial inquiries conducted by Supreme Court judges as well as various administrative probes set up to uncover the truth and punish the guilty, nothing was really 'proved'—neither the government's complicity nor the actions of the guilty individuals. If the struggle for justice failed to secure the conviction of a single political leader or police officer, if all the institutions of the State collapsed so utterly during the carnage of 1984, if the government denied its people a fair and fearless hearing while failing to protect them on those three days where all hell broke loose on the streets of the nation's capital, can we be surprised when we see ourselves lurching from one communal riot to another, with each one being more barbarous and deadly in its intensity?

When I remember those days after so many decades, I wonder about the kind of 'lessons' I have learnt. Along with the mistrust, insecurity, despair, and anger, there is now a new understanding, as well as an empathy and sensitivity for those who are in the minority, or on the periphery, or dispossessed and discriminated against, or still waiting for justice and closure. Much of the work I choose to do now (with writers and social activists in places like Nagaland, Mizoram, Assam, Meghalaya) is an engagement with people who have not been heard, whose voices are still crying out in the dark to challenge an unfair, unseeing and unjust system that continues to deny them a life of dignity and pride.

Perhaps it took the experience of 1984 to bring this home to me.

Why Not A Collective Cry For Justice!

Humra Quraishi

THE VERY WORD 'RIOT' HITS... hits hard! As a young child, I had overheard my maternal grandfather describing rioting in one of the Muslim-populated areas of Uttar Pradesh. Needless to say, those descriptions of anarchy and police brutality on unarmed victims left an impact.

In my adult years, I have witnessed riots erupting and spreading in several regions of the country. I have also seen the condition of the riot survivors – those hapless men and women who have lost everything; even the last ray of hope in the civil administration, in the policing ways, in the speeches of politicians, and in getting timely justice. They sit or squat or survive in a climate of utter hopelessness.

I was residing in New Delhi when two riots ripped off the facade of the State protecting the minority communities of the country. I covered the anti-Muslim riots that broke out in the Seelampur locality soon after the destruction of the Babri Masjid in 1992, and saw for myself the biased role of the police. And during the anti-Sikh riots of 1984, I witnessed horrifying incidents where Sikhs and their properties were targeted by goondas unleashed by the political mafia.

As I recall details of the anti-Sikh riots of 1984, nostalgia overtakes me, pulling me back to the mid-80s. I was residing at New Delhi's Pandara Road, with the Junior Modern School grounds on one side, and Humayun Road on the other end leading to the Ambassador Hotel, Sujan Singh Park and Khan Market. On that particular day when riots erupted in the city, I was home, sitting in the enclosed balcony of my first-floor flat when the telephone rang in that ongoing way.

It was a call from a friend informing me that anti-Sikh riots were spreading in the city and asking me to be careful while going out.

'Why me?' I asked.

'Because you look like a sardarni! What with your long nose, plait, flowing dupattas. Don't step out. You could be attacked.'

My first reaction was that of disbelief. What? Riots! Rioting in New Delhi? Nah! How could rioting occur in prime localities, in sarkari colonies?

Perhaps to settle the pangs of curiosity, I did step out. I walked towards Khan Market and then further on in the direction of the Lodi Gardens, but not beyond that as an eerie quiet had descended... a strange standstill along that entire stretch. I got back home, but before I could introspect on the standstill, the part-time maid cried out that she'd spotted a Sikh man hiding in the hedge along the outer boundary wall. By the time we rushed down the staircase, the man was crawling out of the shrubs along the hedge and running in the direction of the connecting inner lanes. There was a dishevelled look to that wiry man; his long hair was falling all over his face; his clothes were in tatters.

Before we could reach out to him, goon brigades arrived from Humayun Road and started chasing the helpless man in the midst of much chaos and confusion.

As I tried to get in touch with my Sikh friends, the severity of their situation hit me. They were left with only two options: to gather adequate resources to counter the fury of the surcharged mobs, or move out of their homes to so-called safer locales – that is, the homes of their non-Sikh friends.

There was a sense of disbelief together with the outrage. 'Even during Partition, our grandparents and parents didn't suffer this sort of hounding. Like refugees seeking shelter here and there!' one friend fumed.

Another from a supposedly well-connected family said, 'All our connections failed! The loot, the arson, the anarchy continued for hours… made to go on uncontrolled till many more Sikhs could be targeted.'

And, as a senior Sikh bureaucrat's wife recounted, when their sarkari bungalow was besieged by unruly mobs, she was left with little choice but to chop off her young sons' long locks, 'With that non-Sikh look, we were spared but it was all too shocking! A nightmare! No mantris, santris, seepahis, darogas, thanedars came to our rescue. The State was not protecting its own civil servants!'

In recent history, New Delhi had not witnessed bloodshed out in the open, in residential colonies and commercial complexes. The images of burnt homes and shops would linger to haunt for a long time.

The brutality of that rioting affected not just the Sikhs, but everyone who witnessed the havoc and hounding. Years later, when I was interviewing activist Safdar Hashmi's mother, Qamar Azad Hashmi, she told me, 'The 1984 anti-Sikh riots in Delhi affected

Safdar. For days, we were witness to the horrifying carnage. It was shocking to see the brutality of it all. I'd always taught my children never to accept *zulm*... those riots were nothing but *zulm* on innocent people.'

One of the offshoots of the riots was that they brought the Sikhs and Muslims closer. Perhaps, for the first time since Partition, the gap began to shrink between the two communities. Several Sikh friends told me that after experiencing the harsh reality of the anti-Sikh riots, they could understand what the Muslim community goes through each time riots are made to occur in Muslim-populated areas.

In addition to that, the government machinery was exposed to the fullest. While the riots were raging, the cops remained spectators and the political rulers sat mute. According to the late Khushwant Singh, there was a common streak between the 1984 anti-Sikh riots and the 2002 Gujarat riots where the Muslim community was targeted. He commented:

> I witnessed the anti-Sikh riots here in New Delhi and saw for myself the police doing nothing to arrest or even control the rioters. And I have heard from activists and journalists of a similar situation prevailing in the Gujarat carnage of 2002... Yes, there was an apparent similarity between the two. It was obvious that the police had been directed by the political top brass not to control the mobs, the rioters, the looters. In both cases goonda brigades were unleashed to kill and loot, and justice is still waiting for the victims' families.
>
> (From an interview published in *The Indian Express*, 16 April 2003)

The anti-Sikh riots of 1984 dispelled the notion that riots occur or are made to occur only in the small towns, villages and qasbas of the country. In the national capital of India, goon brigades went about unleashing terror in and around prime localities. Furthermore, it wasn't just the economically or socially disadvantaged who got attacked, as was considered the norm in riots. Even the well-to-do and well-connected were targeted. Affluent Sikh families residing in posh South Delhi suburbs were assaulted just as ruthlessly as those living in the East, West or North Delhi neighbourhoods. I heard painful accounts of what went on from several traumatised survivors. Perhaps the most moving is the account of a Sikh carpenter, Balwinder, who lived in Trilokpuri.

A week or so before the rioting, I was introduced to Balwinder, as he sat making dining chairs at a friend's home in Chanakyapuri. I was keen to get a study table and beds made for my children and gave him my telephone number and address. He came to my home to collect the advance money and promised to start working in a couple of days. But then the riots happened. Only after the rioting had subsided did he come. He looked frail and fatigued, as though he'd suffered a nervous breakdown. For hours, he kept recounting the horrors that rioting had heaped on his family. He'd lost not just his home and belongings, but even the will to carry on. His hands trembled, his face was drawn. There was a constant flow of tears as he continued muttering, '*Ajeeb sa mahoul hai… ab kuch bhi ho sakta hai.*' (It is a strange situation… anything can happen.)

Years later, at the launch of journalist-turned-author-turned-politician Jarnail Singh's book, *I Accuse: The Anti-Sikh Violence of 1984*, at the Constitution Club, I saw many riot survivors in the audience. Each one of them carried sorrow in their eyes, in their voices, in their gait… and I was reminded of Balwinder.

Perhaps, there are hundreds of such survivors of the 1984 riots who are 'alive', technically speaking, but not really. The State did not protect them. It killed and wounded psyches, if not bodies. For days, the hapless Sikh masses were terrorised by private senas or goons nurtured by political rulers.

During the course of my interviews with Khushwant Singh, he had talked in detail about the killing of Sikhs, the destruction of their property and the torching of gurudwaras. While talking, he sounded not just pained, but perturbed and upset. To quote him from his essay entitled 'On The '84 Riots' (from *Why I Supported the Emergency: Essays and Profiles*, compiled and edited by Sheela Reddy):

> There are two anniversaries so deeply etched in my mind that every year when they come around I recollect with pain what happened on those days. One is 31 October 1984, when Mrs Gandhi was gunned down by her two Sikh security guards. The other is the following day, when the 'aftermath' consummated itself: frenzied Hindu mobs, driven by hate and revenge, killed nearly 10,000 innocent Sikhs across north India all the way down to Karnataka. In 1989, Mrs Gandhi's assassin, Satwant Singh, and Kehar Singh, a conspirator, paid the penalty for their crime by being hanged to death in Tihar Jail. Twenty-four years later, the killers of 10,000 Sikhs remain unpunished. The conclusion is clear: in secular India there is one law for the Hindu majority, another for Muslims, Christians and Sikhs who are in minority.

In the same essay, Khushwant Singh says,

> 31 October, 1984: The sequence of events remains as vivid as ever. Around 11 a.m., I heard of Mrs Gandhi being shot in her house and taken to hospital. By the afternoon, I heard on the BBC that she was dead. For a couple of hours, life in Delhi came to a standstill. Then hell broke loose—mobs yelling "khoon ka badla khoon se lenge" roamed the streets. Ordinary Sikhs going about their life were waylaid and roughed up. In the evening, I saw a cloud of black smoke billowing up from Connaught Circus: Sikh-owned shops had been put on fire. An hour later, mobs were smashing taxis owned by Sikhs right opposite my apartment. Sikh-owned shops in Khan Market were being looted. Over 100 policemen armed with lathis who lined the road did nothing. At midnight, truckloads of men armed with cans of petrol attacked the gurudwara behind my back garden, beat up the granthi and set fire to the shrine. I was bewildered and did not know what to do. Early next morning, I rang up President Zail Singh. He would not come on the phone. His secretary told me that the president advised me to move into the home of a Hindu friend till the trouble was over. The newly appointed prime minister, Rajiv Gandhi, was busy receiving guests arriving for his mother's funeral; Home Minister Narasimha Rao did not budge from his office; the Lt Governor of Delhi had no orders to put down the rioters. Seventy-two gurudwaras were torched and thousands of Sikh homes looted...
>
> Around mid-morning, a Swedish diplomat came and took my wife and me to his home in the diplomatic enclave... I

> watched Mrs Gandhi's cremation on TV in the home of my Swedish protector... I was a refugee in my own homeland because I was a Sikh.

In the same essay Khushwant Singh goes on to write:

> Symbolic protests did not take long coming. I was part of it; I surrendered the Padma Bhushan awarded to me. Among the people who condemned my action was Vinod Mehta, then the editor of *The Observer*. He wrote that when it came to choosing between being an Indian and a Sikh, I had chosen to be a Sikh. I stopped contributing to his paper. I had never believed that I had to be one or the other. I was both an Indian and a Sikh and proud of being so. I might as well have asked Mehta in return, 'Are you a Hindu or an Indian?' Hindus do not have to prove their nationality; only Muslims, Christians and Sikhs are required to give evidence of their patriotism.

Khushwant Singh was very critical of how the government handled the 1984 riots. In an essay entitled 'On the Nanavati Report', he wrote:

> I have only two words for Justice G.T. Nanavati's inquiry report on the butchery of the Sikhs: utter garbage. I have the report in hand, all 349 pages, plus the Action Taken Report presented by Prime Minister Manmohan Singh's government in Parliament on 8 August, 2005... It is largely based on what transpired in zones of the different police stations and the long lists of names which meant nothing to me. There are broad hints about the involvement of Congress leaders like H.K.L. Bhagat, Jadgish Tytler, Dharam

> Das Shastri and Sajjan Kumar. Nanavati gives them the benefit of the doubt and suggests that yet another inquiry commission look into the charges against them. Yet another commission? For God's sake, is he serious? To say the least, I was deeply disappointed with the whole thing. But the game of shirking responsibility was to attain higher levels!

Disappointment and anger were widespread. None of the politicians and policemen who terrorised the hapless was labelled a terrorist. One was struck by the ruthlessness of the system, by the lack of accountability and transparency, by those divisive ploys and shrewd political tactics. In fact, the 1984 riots threw up a whole new class of so-called 'experts' who continue to hold sway to this day. Each time a riot erupts and havoc spreads, I'm more than shocked to hear a bunch of sarkari or semi-sarkari characters come up with their so called 'expert' comments that reek of bogus declarations and near-teasers in the form of senseless one-liners: 'Riots controlled. All safe and sound. Situation back to normal!' Nah, these men and women, seated inside their air-conditioned official dens, are incapable of visualising how 'normalcy' can ever return when the basic fabric lies ruptured by killings and counter-killings, loot and destruction, illegal arrests and unwarranted detentions, rapes and molestations. Tell me, how can 'normalcy' ever prevail in such surcharged situations?

Debates and discussions on the small screen get equally annoying when politics enters the fray. The conversation revolves around community-wise killings! How many humans attacked or murdered or lynched or roasted alive from this or that community! When I watch television discussions and biased commentaries on riots and attacks on minority groups and communities, I am struck by just how hardened we have become to political murder taking place under various guises. How ruthlessly insensitive we have become in these times! How short-sighted and thick-skinned of us not to ask some pertinent questions.

For instance, why is even one citizen raped or incinerated in the name of religion? Why does the State machinery fail to protect the hapless citizen from the communally-charged mobs? Why do political workers turn into killers? Why does the police machinery get swayed by political dictates? Why are the riots allowed to go on uncontrolled? (This is not to overlook the basic fact that any riot can be controlled by the State machinery, even before it erupts!) Why is the political mafia not exposed?

Today, as the political climate gets murkier and communal poisoning is unleashed in every possible way, it is apparent that the political will has become far too diluted to reach out to the survivors of the 1984 riots awaiting justice. All these years, I have heard my Sikh friends talk of that painful phase. Instead of justice, all they have got is a bagful of bogus political assurances.

Why should the Sikh community alone demand justice for all that was destroyed and demolished during the 1984 riots? Let us raise a collective voice. We, the people of this country, should collectively demand justice for each and every riot victim in this country, irrespective of his or her community.

When Steel Entered My Soul

Rana Chhina

I WRITE THIS NOT TO invoke hate but to rid myself of a burden I have carried for too long.

The year 1984 marked a personal rite of passage. Its events are shrouded inside me behind a veil that I cannot lift. The horror it inflicted was painful and shocking, all the more so because it was unexpected. It was the year that steel entered my soul, compelling me to make a journey I had no wish to undertake. The scar it left was indelible and I still carry it hidden from sight, but known to me for what it is and for what it did to me. Yet it is a dark mark and not one that I wear on my sleeve, for to do so would be to give it an importance that it does not deserve. I fear that doing so will generate hate and allow those that deal in hate to win. To preserve humanity, in the face of inhumanity, must be the guiding principle of human endeavour and the touchstone in narratives of catharsis such as this.

For me 1984 was, in many ways, a Dickensian year. As a young man in love, the cares of the world rested lightly on my shoulders. The girl I loved was in London. My parents were in good health and had finished constructing their house in Delhi. I had just been posted from far-off Hashimara in the Bhutan Duars to Bareilly, just three hours away from home. While flying in the Central Air Command was a bit of a drag compared to the devil-may-care capers of the 'Eastern Air Force' – that was how the rugged and inaccessible areas of north-east India falling within the purview of the Eastern Air Command were known within the Indian Air Force – the central Himalayas from Pithoragarh to Kedarnath provided much relief from the baking plains of Awadh and I spent many days chalking up flying hours in the mountains. It was the best of times. The angry clouds building up in the west over the Punjab seemed far away and appeared to be just another rumble in the eternal turbulence of the Indian political landscape. As Sikhs, with close ties to the Punjabi heartland – our village lies in the Majha, near Amritsar – we were concerned about the escalating violence and uncertainty. Yet we were, like the majority of the Sikhs, invested whole-heartedly in the idea of India as a secular, democratic nation. Operation Blue Star and the widening communal divide had, however, shaken us, as it had shaken a number of Hindus who did not subscribe to the divisive politics giving rise to the forces of communalism.

Like many Punjabis of their generation, my parents were refugees. Caught up in the greatest mass migration in human history, they had been uprooted from the land of their birth. When India awoke to freedom and its tryst with destiny on the stroke of the midnight hour on 15 August 1947, the people of the Punjab – Hindu, Muslim and Sikh – woke up to horror and suffering caused by an unscrupulous betrayal of trust by colonial Britain and an unconscionable compromise by India's political elite. For the Punjab, and the Punjabi diaspora of my parents' generation, 15 August 1947 was always 'Partition' instead of

'Independence'. Growing up in a Punjabi household in Delhi in the 1960s, the inevitable follow-up question the house elders put to a new acquaintance after the initial 'and where are you from?' was always, 'Par pichhon kithon aye si?' (But from where do you originate?).

I never heard a word of bitterness or reproach from my parents or from my uncles in the village, even though they lost everything in the upheaval of 1947. My father was a professor of physiology at the All India Institute of Medical Sciences (AIIMS). Like many of his contemporaries, he was a man of strong principles and high ideals. Our cultural moorings, and those of his friends, Hindu and Sikh alike, were syncretic and secular. There was no room for the narrow-minded or the ultra-conservative in my parents' circle of friends and acquaintances. I grew up in a middle-class household, unburdened by the strictures of conservative society though not unaware of them.

I am an only child. In 1977, I left home to join the National Defence Academy, that 'maker of men'. In 1981, I was commissioned in the Indian Air Force and assigned to the helicopter stream as I had excessive 'sitting height' for flying fighters. I spent the first three years of my service career flying the single-engine Chetak (Allouette) helicopter in the East and in the Central Himalayas. In the summer of 1984, I was sent to Gauhati to commence my technical conversion to the twin-engined Mi-8 (Pratap) helicopter along with three other youngsters from my unit. The three-month long course passed all too soon and came to an end on 26 October 1984. The next step was to proceed to Bangalore to carry out our flying conversion on the aircraft. As luck would have it, a Packet C-119 was returning to its base at Agra and two of us, Flying Officer

Radha Shankar and I, decided to hitch a ride in it. That would give us a few bonus days at my home in Delhi and we could then proceed by train to Bangalore on the 2nd to reach in time for the course commencing at Yelahanka on 5 November. At least, that was the plan.

The flight to Agra was uneventful, although I recall being slightly disconcerted while looking down through a gap in the fuselage near the clamshell doors and seeing the earth a few thousand feet below. From Agra, we managed to catch a bus to Delhi and made our way to my house in the AIIMS campus where my parents, who were pleasantly surprised to see us, greeted us warmly.

On 30 October, my father drove me to the Air HQ to see an officer and enquire about my next posting. We went back there again on the morning of the 31st, the day Prime Minister Indira Gandhi was shot. When we returned around mid-day, the news was out. The initial news bulletins reported her condition as critical and said that she had been shot by two of her guards who had surrendered their weapons afterwards. Soon after that, however, it was announced that one of her guards had been shot dead and the other was severely wounded. Both of them were Sikhs and had shot her for what they saw as her complicity in the attack on the Golden Temple in June that year. The bulletin also announced that she had been taken to the AIIMS casualty.

In those days, my father would walk back home from his department for lunch. As we sat down to eat that afternoon, he said that he had heard from his colleagues that Mrs Gandhi was no more, but the announcement was not going to be made right then. The talk turned to the act of assassination. This was an act of passion; the desecration of the holiest shrine of the Sikh faith by the Indian state had shaken Sikhs all over the world to their core. It hearkened a collective memory back to similar acts of desecration under the worst Mughal persecution two centuries ago and many Sikhs felt that the assassination was a justifiable act of retribution for an unforgivable act that struck at the very core of their belief.

I asked my father what he thought of this. His reply was characteristic of the man. He said that she was the elected prime minister of the nation, and in his opinion her killing was just as unjustifiable as her actions.

After lunch, round 3.30 p.m., Shankar and I strolled down from my house at C-II/7 to the main gate of the hospital in front of the private ward. By now a large crowd had gathered there and people were milling about, talking in hushed tones. There were some Sikhs in the crowd as well. After a while, we returned home. Shortly after that, my father came back from office at 5 p.m. and decided to go shopping. As he approached the campus gate on Ring Road, he was stopped by a nurse who had happened to assist in my delivery at the time of my birth. She told him that mobs were targeting Sikhs all over the city and advised him to go back home. As he turned back, a policeman who was standing near a police jeep and had overheard the conversation, also called out to repeat the nurse's advice. 'They are killing the Sardars,' he said. 'We are keeping even our saathis (companions) out of sight.' He lifted the flap of the jeep to reveal a couple of Sikh constables in uniform hiding inside.

My father returned home and we spent the next eight or nine days in a mixture of disbelief, anxiety, fear and anger. I am unsure of the sequence of what transpired during that time, or even of the time frame. I think that it was eight or nine days. It may have been more, or less. I do not know. I do not want to know.

Many years later, I received a phone call from a young man, a journalist, who asked how I was, how my parents were. When I said that I had not placed him, he said, 'But don't you remember? You saved my life in 1984.' He said he was being chased by a mob when I offered him a lift on my scooter and brought him home. I racked my brains, and did recall that we sheltered a young man in our house for about five days but I cannot for the life of me remember the circumstances in which I saved him.

My mother, who was a great admirer of Pandit Nehru, was genuinely upset to see Indira Gandhi dead. The television and the radio were our link to the 'outside' world and we followed the news closely. Over the next few days, we heard horrifying stories. Mobs led by Congressmen had stopped buses on the Safdarjung flyover, pulled out Sikhs travelling in them, and flung them onto the tracks below. In other places, they were placing rubber tyres around the necks of their victims and setting them alight. Some people spoke of 'teaching the Sikhs a lesson', and I remember watching the TV in disbelief as Rajiv Gandhi made his abhorrent comment: 'when a big tree falls, the earth will shake', to justify the genocide taking place around him.

Shankar stayed on for a day and then decided to leave by train for Bangalore. Even though it meant that I would go AWOL, we decided that I should not accompany him, but stay at home to venture out only after things settled down. As it turned out, he was to witness the train being stopped on the outskirts of Delhi and Sikhs dragged out and butchered by marauding mobs. I remember that a promising young officer, who was supposed to go to France for his test pilot's course, was murdered in Palam.

On the third or fourth day, shortly after the Army was called out to restore law and order, we received a call from Sheila Mehta, the wife of my father's lifelong friend and veteran journalist, Balraj Mehta. The Mehtas resided in Gulmohar Park and knew that the Army was camping in the AIIMS campus. Mrs Mehta said that a mob was gathering in front of a Sikh residence near their house and wanted me to tell the Army to come to their rescue. I put on my uniform and for the first time in four days stepped out of the house and marched to the AIIMS Guest House where a Gurkha unit had set up camp. For the first time in my life, I was conscious of my physical identity as a Sikh. As I passed the sentry at the Guest House gate, he did not salute. I walked past him and entered the Guest House where the officers were eating their lunch. I sought out the senior-most officer there and went up to him. After saluting him, I informed him of the purpose of my visit. He said he would see to it as soon as he had finished lunch. However, since lives were at stake, I persisted. He looked at me wearily and said he would leave in a few minutes. As I left, I heard him calling for his jeep.

The campus was relatively safe; a haven of tranquility in a city on fire. Yet, a day or so later, someone came and said that a mob had entered the campus and asked us to be prepared for the worst. I pulled out the two small swords that I had inherited from my mother's family. The larger one was made in 1947 as communal riots escalated, while the smaller sword was made from the blade of my maternal grandfather's cavalry sabre, which was broken during an engagement in Mesopotamia during the First World War. A hilt had been attached to it in 1947. It was steel born of violence and had seen my family through turbulent times before and I hoped it would do so once again. I also pulled out my father's two licensed firearms: a .32 Smith & Wesson revolver and a 12 bore Winchester repeater. As I loaded the weapons and kept the spare ammunition handy on a nearby table, I slipped three cartridges into my pocket; one each for my parents and the last one for myself. If all else failed, I was determined that we would not be taken alive by the mob. Luckily, the mob was turned back and a few days later the city limped back to 'normal'. As we emerged cautiously into the open, I was not aware of the change that had occurred deep within my sub-conscious. It was only a few years ago, when my parents finally passed away that I realised how deeply the iron had entered my soul and the change it had wrought. From being a mild and passive individual, I was now someone ever ready to react with aggression. 1984 was the passage of innocence. It left me wound up like a coiled spring and I have not as yet fully confronted the horrors of that nightmarish time where people were willing to kill me merely for who I was and what I represented.

There are other fragments that I can unearth from the graveyard of buried memories. My parents had just constructed a house. It was still empty and the caretaker had managed to prevent a mob from damaging it by ripping off the name plate and insisting that it belonged to a Hindu. The elderly Sikh carpenter and his sons, who had done the woodwork in the house, were not so lucky. They lived in the notorious Trilokpuri colony in East Delhi where the police connived with the lumpen gangs in the systematic massacre of the Sikh residents. They were dragged out of their houses and killed with all the refinements that the Delhi mob could muster. I recall the carpenter as a gentle man with polite sons.

My father's friend, the renowned orthopedic surgeon Dr PS Maini, who lived in South Extension, was only able to escape with his life by being transported in the boot of his car. In every corner of the city, for months afterwards, the signs of the violence lingered, whether in the burnt out husks of houses or shops, or in the indelible marks on the road near the Laxmi Nagar crossing that were caused by the hundreds of gallons of paint looted from a Sikh business and poured onto the street in front.

There were other effects as well. My mother never quite recovered from the trauma of the riots and her fear was one of the main factors in persuading my father to move to the United States after his retirement. In the Air Force, for nearly a decade after the riots, Sikh officers were not posted to the Air HQ Communication Squadron, which flew VVIPs, or assigned to similar VIP flights.

Luckily, there was no backlash against Hindus living in rural Punjab, although many left in the ensuing years of terrorist uncertainty. Life gradually limped back to normal. I quickly realised that it was futile to try and explain what I had gone through to those who were not there. Friends were sympathetic, but were unable to fathom the extent of the trauma that the experience had caused. In order to survive, it was important to try to forget. However, nearly seven years later when my wife woke me up from a nap to announce that Rajiv Gandhi had been killed, my first words were, 'Where is the revolver?' My relief that he had not been killed by a Sikh was immense.

In hindsight, I feel that there is more good than evil in this world. In the worst of times, the vast majority of Hindus never lost their sense of decency or allowed their balance to be swayed by the base instincts of the mob. The fabric of Indian society, which embodies the best qualities of human nature, held. By doing so, it gave hope to many of us that what had happened was nothing but an orchestrated aberration of the worst kind.

Subsequent events in Gujarat, though, have shown that we have not yet learnt our lessons and that the body politic of our nation is yet to mature to its full potential. Those of us who toil to build the social edifice of this country have, to paraphrase Robert Frost, many miles to go before we can sleep.

In Imagination

When Big Trees Fall

NS Madhavan
Translated from the original Malayalam by NP Ashley

WHENEVER I CHECK THE REGISTERS of the monastery one thing surprises me. Most number of deaths here happen during the November-December months. In these cold months, the decrepit hearts of the aged inmates of the monastery perhaps stop to function in the struggle to give them heat.

In this October, there was only one death – Sister Philomena's. When Sister Philomena wasn't seen during breakfast, I asked, 'What happened to Philomenamma?'

Sister Katrina rolled her wheelchair away from the dining table and sat under the pointed arch of the window. The counting of the rosary beads in the hands of Sister Margaritta became faster. Sister Martha drank milk drop by drop, keeping her head down. I didn't need to go and see Sister Philomena in the long hall with beds on both sides. I called up Father Thomas of the Bishop's house and asked him to come down immediately.

I clearly remember 1984, October 31. That morning I went

to the Meerut railway station. A nun was arriving from Orissa to become an inmate in the monastery. By the time we reached, the train had already arrived. Seeing me, two people, a young nun and an aged nun with tiny wrinkles spread all over her face, stepped forward.

'Sister, are you a Malayali?' the aged nun asked me almost immediately.

'Yes.'

'Where in Kerala?'

'Varappuzha. Near Ernakulam. Where are you from, Mother?'

'I am from the north. Thiruvambady. My father had migrated from the south of Kerala to the north.'

The young nun was from Orissa. She had to go back the next day itself. Sister Angelica – that was the name of the old nun. The young nun told me that Sister Angelica was diabetic and hence she shouldn't be given anything sweet. 'I was in Orissa throughout my life,' said Sister Angelica. 'Cuttack, Rourkela, Kalahandi and last, Bhubaneswar. I was teaching Mathematics and Science. And finally, I arrive here in Meerut. Doesn't everything end here?' she said on our way to the monastery, turning back at the cemetery dense with crosses.

This monastery for aged nuns was founded by the bishop who passed away last year. Earlier, nuns used to spend their old age in the place they had been working and living. A complaint kept surfacing in the bishop's meetings that they weren't given adequate care.

When I returned from Germany after my higher studies in nursing, the then bishop of Meerut sent for me.

'You are a child of the Church.' The Bishop, who was from Changanassery, knew of my growing up in the orphanage, of

God's calling at a young age, and of the Church sending me to Germany for higher studies.

'I thought of this monastery keeping you in mind. A haven for our aged nuns who can no longer do God's work. You should run it.'

I didn't sleep through that night. Since childhood, my mediator on such occasions was Gabriel, the angel of angels. I prayed for a long time. At last, I heard the flapping of wings behind me. The messenger of God had come. 'Oh, the one close to God, Jesus built the Holy Church on the rock of Peter. Can the monastery sustain on me, this fragile white pebble?'

'Sister Agatha,' my own mind whispered in the voice of Gabriel. 'This is the Almighty giving you an opportunity to be the salt of the earth.'

Oh salt, that has lost its sourness, I cried with my face pressed on the bed.

From the first group of inmates in the monastery, only Sister Karuna is alive now. Sister Karuna, a native of Spain, used to run a training centre for destitute girls in Bihar. She came to the monastery with a grand piano.

By the time I allotted the bed and arranged other things for Sister Angelica, it was eleven. It was then that Father Thomas from Bishop's house called, 'Did you hear? Apparently, Indira Gandhi has been shot.'

'Oh God!' I was petrified.

'Everybody says she is dead. But the radio is still reporting that she is only injured.'

'Jesus Christ,' Sister Angelica said when she got to know the news. 'She was in Orissa the day we were starting from there.'

While feeding her light-green soup with a spoon, I told Sister Davis. 'Indira Gandhi has been shot.'

The mind of Sister Davis had flown away like a bird a couple of years ago. She said nothing other than opening her mouth for the next sip.

Sister Karuna went and sat near her piano when she heard the news. Its open lid gave her asylum like a tree. She sat flipping through the song books, without playing the piano. At two, Father Thomas called again, 'Radio Australia has announced that Indira Gandhi is dead. Some newspapers in Delhi have also brought out one-page editions.'

'AIR?'

'They are still saying she is injured.'

'TV?'

'They too.'

When I got out of the phone-room, I saw Sister Katrina reading the prayer book while sitting in the wheelchair. I told her in Malayalam, 'Did you hear? Father Thomas called up and said Indira Gandhi has been shot dead.'

Sister Katrina had almost stopped talking after the death of Philomenamma. They both had came to the monastery from Delhi together. She lifted her face, trying to ask something, but was defeated by the struggle to form words. She pushed the wheelchair into the inner room. I noted in my mind that it was time to oil its wheels.

When I reached the office room, I saw Sister Margarita hovering near the open almirah stealthily.

'Sister,' I said in an admonishing tone. 'What are you doing?'

'Nothing.'

'Lie. Aren't you looking for the medicines so that you could throw them away?'

It was the gardener who found out that Sister Margarita was throwing away the blood pressure tablets she was supposed to have thrice a day. Seeing red and blue tablets trapped in chrysanthemum plants and petals of dahlia flowers, he was amazed. When he picked them up and showed them to me, I immediately understood these were Sister Margarita's tablets. From that day onwards, I made sure that she had her medicines in my presence.

Suddenly, Sister Martha came into the office room. Noting how agile she was, I often wondered whether she reached Meerut a little too early.

'Is the news true?'

'Mmm.'

'How sad! Indira Gandhi had once come to address a meeting in Indore at the ground of the school I used to teach in. She threw the garlands and bouquets she got to the children. She apparently did that all the time. Adivasi boys, on their bare feet, ran around deftly catching them. Indira got excited. She started extracting flowers from bouquets and tossed them. But the smart children didn't allow a single one to fall on the ground.'

At nightfall, the news that Indira Gandhi had been killed came on TV for the first time.

That night very few inmates came to the dining room for dinner. The ninety-six-year-old Sister Mary, who usually has her meals sitting in bed, came leaning on a walking stick to the dining hall, 'I want to sit with everybody else. It has been a long time,' she smiled.

Sister Davis, who had grown senile, sat staring into the

TV set without muttering to herself. Sister Katrina rolled her wheelchair away from the TV.

Sister Martha was crying, 'I can't forget the volley ball with the bouquets.'

Nuns lay down to sleep in the red glow of room heaters. I switched off the light in my room on the first floor after saying my prayers. I was shivering under the woollen blanket. This shiver was not due to the November cold; it was my share in the fever that had caught the nation.

After some time I heard somebody knocking on the door. When I opened the door, Sister Sicily who accompanied Sister Angelica was standing outside.

'Sister Agatha,' she said. 'I feel scared.'

I looked into the foggy night behind her. It lay like the sea created at the beginning of the world. It was silent. God had not put a voice in its throat.

'Sister, you can sleep in my room.'

The next morning, Father Thomas from the Bishop's house phoned, 'Trouble has started. Sikhs are getting massacred in groups. Lock up the doors properly. The sister from Orissa shouldn't go back now.'

The Gothic doors and windows were all shut. Sister Sicily, Sister Angelica and Sister Katrina sat around a room heater warming their hands. Sister Mary was lying down hugging a hot water bag. All of them were looking at the hospital room off and on, as they could hear Sister Wilfred wheezing. When the sound increased, I got up and went to give her oxygen from the cylinder.

Gunshots sounded outside. When I looked out at the city from my room on the first floor, I could see frozen trees of smoke. By evening the trees of smoke became a great forest.

The watchman, a Gurkha, sat inside, after having locked up the iron gates. He kept giving news about what was happening outside.

All the shops of the sardars in Clock Tower had been destroyed. The taxis of sardars were being set on fire by the rioters. The dead bodies of sardars could be seen on the way to Sadar Bazaar.

Gunshots could be heard throughout the night. Like sky glow brooding over faraway cities, the red luminescence of fire could be seen in the horizon.

The next day, 2 November, the sound of gunshots only increased. The inmates spent the day in the hall. Even the face of Sister Davis, who had lost her mind, had fear spread all over it.

The next day, we saw the last journey of Indira Gandhi on television. Young Sister Sicily kept describing the scenes to ninety-six-year-old Sister Mary who couldn't see very well.

'The crowd is quite small,' Sister Angelica said. 'People might not have come out fearing attacks. Nehru's funeral procession was something to see. I was in Delhi then.'

Sister Sicily continued her narration based on the TV visuals. Other than Sister Mary, Sister Martha and Sister Margarita sat around her to hear the commentary.

Now, through Delhi's Vijay Chowk, Indira Gandhi's funeral procession was moving. The visual was the same in two dimensions on the TV. Sister Sicily translated the TV images into words. I couldn't take the same tragedy enacted in three platforms. My entrails started stretching heavily. I bent to the washbasin and vomited. Thus, for the first time in life, history touched me physically.

On 4 November, curfew was declared. The inmates stayed

in their beds the whole day. Sister Sicily and I took food to their beds.

At night, Sister Katrina pushed her wheelchair up to me and said, 'I want to go out to the verandah.'

'No sister, you shouldn't.'

'Aren't the lights off? I want to go out. I am feeling suffocated.

'Okay, I will also come with you then.'

Even as they heard the hinges of doors squeaking, the inmates didn't raise their heads to look. The wind through the open doors pierced cold holes in the room's brooding heat.

'Let me walk around a bit,' Sister Katrina said. She moved the wheelchair to the other side of the verandah and back. I stood pressing my face into the darkness.

I got a shock when I heard Sister Katrina's sudden cry from the other side of the verandah. 'Oh Lord, murderers.' The wheelchair came rushing at me sounding like the wheels of a train.

Sister Katrina was gasping, 'Murderers in the darkness…'

I ran to the kitchen. Sister Karuna swiftly came out and locked the door after pushing Sister Katrina's wheelchair inside. I selected the sharpest of the knives and hid it under my clothes.

The sisters were silent. Inside the hospital room, Sister Wilfred was struggling to reduce the sound of wheezing by pulling back her muscles. Then we heard somebody banging on the door. Sister Karuna and Sister Martha stood touching me. The banging got louder.

'Open, please open,' a woman was heard saying in Hindi. A child's cry followed.

We could hear motorcycles roaring up and halting outside the monastery. Their headlights ran around the walls like the searchlights of a circus.

'Open, they have come to get me,' the woman was wailing.

When I opened the door, we could see a woman clad in a salwar kameez with her head covered by a shawl and a Sikh boy who had his hair tied up with a white handkerchief.

'They killed my husband. They killed my elder son Bablu. They are saying they will kill me. And this boy too,' she said, teetering on the ridges of madness.

When those motorcycle riders started pounding on the gate of the monastery, Sister Karuna ushered the woman and the child inside and locked the door. Until the gang of motorcycle riders left the place, saying something to the Gurkha, nobody spoke a word.

'Who are you?' Sister Martha broke the silence in Hindi.

'My name is Amarjeet. They killed many people in our colony. As a protest against the Army's entry into the Harmandir Sahib, the Sikhs of our colony didn't celebrate Diwali this year. That was why they were so terribly angry with us.'

'Didn't the policemen come for your help?'

'The police station is right in front of our colony. The people in the colony had gone to meet the station in-charge. He said he couldn't do anything as there weren't enough police personnel. He also hated us.'

'Then?' Sister Martha continued.

'We left our homes and moved to the gurudwaras.'

Nihang Sikhs who wore blue clothes and blue turbans with quoits of steel kept vigil outside gurudwaras. The singers sang the praises of the Guru, accompanied by harmoniums hung from their shoulders. Kirpans, the daggers worn by the Sikhs, were hanging from everybody's waist. Some had guns too.

Adi Granth, the Sikh holy book, sat on a stool covered with a red silk cloth. The granthis respectfully waved the yak-hair fans over it. Devotees dropped coins in front of it. At a corner of the gurudwara, the devotees were heaping up wheat flour for the *langar,* the common kitchen.

Only one Akali from Gurdaspur gave a speech: Khalsapanth, the community of initiated Sikhs, needs blood today. The blood of the Guru's own Sikhs. Oh Sikhs, oh, you who had been baptised by the *amrit,* to be immortal even while dying for the Guru, what the Guru needs is sacrifice, sacrifice. In the blood of the listeners, the genes that carried the clan's memories swam around. All of them called out loud: Sat sri akal!

'When policemen started their rounds, some of us returned home. Others stayed back in the camp of the gurudwara.'

The attack took place at night. They picked up Amarjeet's husband selectively and killed him. Then the elder son. A man clutched on to Amarjeet's hand. When she savaged his flesh with her teeth, he had to let her go.

'I ran dragging my boy,' she said. 'I remember the face of the man who grasped my hand. Ramji. My husband has an iron store at the junction. Ramji has been trying to snatch it somehow for a while now. If both of us are finished off, he can have the shop.'

They spent an entire day in the gurudwara. But Ramji and his friends were circling around the gurudwara on bikes and jeeps. Policemen must have been bought off by them. Once it got dark, Amarjeet and her son ran out stealthily from the gurudwara. At night, stepping through the gaps in the wall of the monastery, they entered the compound.

Sister Sicily brought a cup full of milk and gave it to the boy. He drank it in one go.

'What is his name?' Sister Angelica asked.

'Joginder Singh. We call him Juggy at home.'

'Do you want more milk?' Sister Katrina asked him.

Juggy nodded yes, unabashedly. Sister Martha got a glassful of milk, bread and a couple of boiled eggs from the kitchen.

'We have no hope here. We have to leave this place,' Amarjeet said. 'We have to go to Delhi. I have relatives in the camp in Fatehpur gurudwara. Can we stay here till we manage to escape to Delhi?'

Oh Jesus, you give us opportunities to be compassionate. I took Amarjeet's hand and led her to the now vacant bed of Sister Philomena, who died in October.

'You can sleep here,' I said. Then I prepared the bed on the floor for Juggy. After eating a long loaf of bread alone, he slipped into a sleep in which he was unlikely to see any dream. The sisters also went to bed after saying their prayers.

Next morning, 5 November, the sisters got up earlier than usual. I thought they were waiting for Juggy to wake up.

Juggy's attention first went to Sister Karuna who looked different from the other nuns. Her light blue eyes amazed him. Sister Karuna walked to the piano holding his hands. He stood looking at the black and white keys. Sister Karuna pressed on one key. 'Do,' she said.

Hesitantly, Juggy also pressed the same key, 'Do.' The inmates of the monastery heard the voice of Juggy for the first time.

'Re, Mi, Fa,' Sister Karuna said rhythmically pressing the keys.

Sister Angelica went to Juggy smiling. She pressed on the hair tied with a white handkerchief. Then she looked at me and said, 'Doesn't this look like a spider's egg?'

Juggy's face went red. He forcibly removed Sister Angelica's hand. He was so agitated that he even pushed her away from him. From that moment, Juggy's hair became off-limits for us. We understood that the historical sense of a clan lay braided in that.

Sister Margarita asked for her medicines that day. Sister Katrina hovered around Amarjeet and Juggy in her wheelchair. Sister Karuna got busy baking a cake for Juggy.

I contacted the Bishop's House to take permission for allowing Amarjeet and Juggy to stay at the monastery. Father Thomas said he would consult the bishop and call me back. Even before I started thinking whether the bishop would agree or not, the phone started ringing.

'The bishop's order is to go ahead on the path shown by God,' Father Thomas said.

As it was curfew time, the doors and windows of the monastery were kept open without fear. After years, the ninety-six-year-old Sister Mary got out into the garden. One end of her walking stick was held by Juggy. Through Sister Mary's cataract, sunlight lay bleary like the Milky Way.

'What is the name of this flower?' Juggy asked.

'What does it look like?'

'Like the moon. Round and big.'

'Colour?'

'Yellow.'

'Does it have many petals?' Sister Mary asked.

'Petals? Yes, much more than lotuses have. Small, not-so-broad petals.'

'Then the name of this flower is dahlia.'

Sister Mary and Juggy moved to the next flower. Sisters looked at them curiously from the verandahs. While they were climbing back into the monastery, Sister Mary said, looking at everybody, gasping and with a smile, 'Juggy has become Adam, by christening all objects, moving and unmoving today.'

The next day there was a relaxation in the curfew. Trains started running. We sent Sister Sicily, who had to go back to Orissa, Amarjeet and Juggy to the railway station with the Gurkha. When they were at the steps, Sister Wilfred came out of the hospital room. 'Juggy, Juggy,' she called out loud, and placed an engraved locket of the Virgin Mary in Juggy's hand. He took it, waved at everyone one last time and ran to join his mother.

Just as life was getting back to normal in the monastery, a military vehicle came and stopped outside the compound. From it, the Gurkha, Amarjeet, Sister Sicily and Juggy climbed out. Juggy stood motionless with his eyes closed. Sister Sicily made him walk holding his hands. As soon as they entered the monastery, he disappeared somewhere.

'What happened?' I asked. The Gurkha narrated the story.

'We had walked only some distance. A jeep came and stopped near us. A person jumped out of the jeep to grab memsaab. By then Juggy had started crying "Ma, Ma, those people, those people." The mother and son started to run.'

'They had been lying in wait for us for hours,' Amarjeet said sobbing.

'They sped up the jeep to chase them and run them over.' Though the Gurkha was shivering with fear, the ability of his Mongolian features – contracted eyes, joined eye brows and sharp jaws – to express emotion was limited.

'Luckily they were saved because an Army vehicle arrived right then,' said the Gurkha.

'Don't worry,' Sister Karuna said. Sister Martha found Juggy sitting quietly under the stairs in the darkness.

'You can live here for as many days as you want. Nothing will happen to you,' I said.

The words of this sinner, uttered without the consent of the Almighty, had already gone astray. I got a call: 'CIA agents, if you don't leave the sardarni and child for us, we will bomb your monastery out of existence.' Before I could say 'hello, hello' with my parched throat, he had hung up.

Though the police force was deployed to give protection, stones were pelted at the rear of the monastery. One of the stones hit the stained glass painting of Jesus with a sheep. It broke the heart of the shepherd.

The next day, on 7 November, Father Thomas called early in the morning from the Bishop's House. 'They have demolished the statue of Our Lady of the Lourdes outside St. Mary's School. They are calling up frequently asking for custody of the sardarni and the child.'

'Will the unrest turn against *us*?' I asked.

Father Thomas didn't say anything.

'What should I do?'

'Bishop said God will continue to show you the way ahead.'

I went and knelt down in the prayer room. Angel Gabriel, give me a message. Don't you have any message for me from God? Other than shadows moving ahead through the frontiers of the mind like a train of refugees, nothing else came to mind.

My mind was empty. I started weeping. After sometime, I felt an ethereal peace. By then, Amarjeet and the other inmates reached the prayer room.

I asked the driver of the ambulance, George, to bring a coffin.

The road that God showed to this sinner was this, I said looking at the inmates. Amarjeet will wear the habit of a nun.

Juggy will lie in the coffin inside the ambulance. Some of us will stand around praying. We will get into the eastern gate of the cemetery in a way people can see and drive out of the western gate. Then we will reach the church near the railway station. It won't be difficult to get to the railway station from there.

Sister Sicily went out of the room and brought Juggy there. Sister Angelica held his hands tightly. Sister Martha sat down on the floor and pressed down his legs. Even then Juggy was trying to free himself ferociously like an animal. Sister Mary created a trap for his knee with the crooked side of the walking stick. Sister Margarita closed his eyes with her hand. When he started crying out loud, Sister Karuna covered his mouth with her hand.

Amarjeet removed the white handkerchief from Juggy's hair. I untied his hair that was tied to the crown of his head. It stretched down to his shoulders. I sprinkled water to make it damp and then with a big pair of scissors, started cutting his hair. As strands of hair fell on to the floor of the monastery, he became more and more naked.

'Waheguru wahe,' Amarjeet whimpered.

Juggy's helplessness grew. He stopped crying. Sister Karuna withdrew her hand from his mouth.

'Jo bole so nihaal,' Amarjeet said to lead Juggy.

'Sat sri akal,' Juggy said mechanically. By that time his hair had become very short.

I noticed the skin-colour change on his face only after the haircut. The part that came under the head cover, as it hadn't seen sunlight for years, had a different colour and shape. That would definitely give him away. Mixing charcoal in mustard oil, I made a paste and smeared it on his face to make the colour look identical across his face.

The ambulance had reached by then. In the coffin inside the ambulance, Juggy lay down. The coffin was closed in such a way that air could get in. Amarjeet, in the garb of a nun, Sister Sicily who was going back to Orissa, Sister Angelica, Sister Karuna, Sister Martha and I sat around the coffin to cover it and started saying our prayers.

Initially the journey was calm. After some time motorcycles came racing towards us. They rode the bikes parallel to George and asked him to stop. George started driving faster. We had the motorcycles roaring behind us, changing gears quickly. Sister Karuna placed her long hand on George's shoulder and asked him to stop.

She opened the back door of the ambulance and stood at the step. Her veil, caught in the wind, flew like hair left open. Her blue irises, with dark pupils contracted to pinpoints, confused motor cyclists. Holding up the hand with the thurible, Sister Karuna asked in Hindi, 'Satans, won't you spare even the dead?'

Sister Angelica and I increased the speed of the Malayalam prayer song we were singing. After hesitating for a minute, the motorcyclists went away. We went through the cemetery and got out of the other gate. The journey up to the church near the railway station was event-free. When the ambulance stopped, Amarjeet and I opened the lid of the coffin.

'Get up, Juggy,' Amarjeet said. Just like a butterfly coming out of its pupa, he got up. He ran his hands through his hair with the sorrow of broken clan-continuity. The knowledge that the hair I cut off sprouted in his mother's womb started suffocating me.

Amarjeet, Sister Sicily and Juggy got into the women's compartment of the train. He stood pressing the window panes of the train. Without him realising it, his hands went to his head.

The next day the riots practically ended. There was no curfew during the day. Sister Mary didn't get up from her bed. Sister Margarita moved her wheelchair as far as possible from everybody else. Sister Margarita refused to take her medicines. Sister Angelica tried talking of old matters. Sister Davis lay murmuring. Sister Karuna sat in front of the piano doing nothing. Sister Martha prayed throughout the day. Sister Wilfred returned to the hospital room.

As for me, I went to the prayer room and locked myself in, with the experience of the deaths foretold in November hanging heavily in the air like static electricity.

The Perished and the Saved

Jaspreet Singh

I, RAJ KUMAR, FIRST ENCOUNTERED him in 1984, not in a classroom, but in the student residence.

My mother had accompanied me to the red-brick residence with two items of luggage (a black trunk and a roll of bedding), and she had ventured beyond the visitor's lounge. She wanted to test the quality of the food in the hostel canteen, and there Professor Singh, the boys' hostel warden, spotted her.

To this day, for some unknown reason, I am unable to forget his accent and choice of words, which conveyed three or four crucial years spent abroad. British, American, Indian English, strands no longer distinct, fuzzy, like a superposition of sine and cosine waves. Even his majestic turban looked westernised.

Slowly he walked up towards Mother; his yellow tie fluttering in the wind, 'May I be of assistance?' Gently, he reassured her and joked, 'If your boy doesn't like the spartan food here, he could always eat at my place.'

A few months after joining the engineering college in Delhi, the exact day I topped the class, Professor Singh extended an invitation: 'If you are free this evening, you are most welcome to dine at Nelly and my place.'

The family lived in Munirka, only a kilometre outside the college. Those days, there were fewer houses and shops and people in the area and it was possible to walk real fast. Their front garden was filled with voluptuous bougainvillea and purple-blossomed jacarandas.

Hesitantly, I rang the bell. I was late by a full hour; I apologised. I could not reveal the real reason for the delay. Accompanied by a bunch of classmates, I had gone to Chanakya to watch my first adult film. Plus, the campus gift shop was closed to mark an optional religious holiday, and I felt embarrassed arriving empty-handed. Hesitantly, I rang the bell. The bookshelves and other objects in the house suggested this family was steeped in deep knowledge about the world.

Nelly was perhaps the most beautiful woman I had ever encountered – a serene Sikh beauty, and the most refined. She would call him 'MN' with a sense of ease that Indian wives of that generation didn't normally possess. (MN or 'em en' stood for Mohan and was the best chemical tease.)

She greeted me with a sardonic smile. In fact, both Nelly and Professor Singh had the same smile.

She had studied literature at a state college in Punjab, and was much younger, only eight or nine years older than me; they had married after he returned from Cornell University. When I arrived at the house she was playing a musical instrument, a rabab. Her two children, both boys with long hair, were asleep in the bedroom.

In our class she was known as Mrs Singh, everybody fancied the khoobsurat sardarni. Until that evening, I had only seen the enigmatic Nelly from a distance. I will never forget the bread pakoras she fried, not with dhaniya and tamarind, but with what she called cranberry chutney. That was the first time I tasted cranberries. There was a layer of spicy potatoes in the pakoras. She served channa-kulcha as well, and cashew burfi and chiki as dessert.

The professor seemed more relaxed that night, he unfolded his beard, and loosened his navy blue turban. Two or three strands of grey in his robust beard. Nelly had on Ella Fitzgerald songs and now and then she would step out of the house, and this seemed to annoy him but he didn't express his annoyance properly. After dinner, Professor Singh did something unusual. He washed the dishes.

Nelly retired to her room without wishing us goodnight, and I ended up discussing dimensionless numbers, all night long, with my teacher. By the time I left, both of us sensed a new layer of relationship emerging, one that is commonly known as friendship. Before departing he also showed me his study. The walls had developed cracks and the electrical wiring was visible. The left side was covered with awards, and commendations, and important citations. On the right wall, hung a huge black-and-white photo of the so-called great leader. She had imposed Emergency in my unfortunate country only six or seven years earlier.

These days, the *Times* often runs profiles of highly qualified immigrants returning to India. Better jobs, better quality of life. Good life in Bangalore or the Los Angeles-style Millennium City, Gurgaon. To me, these returns are not even half as interesting as Professor Singh's decision to return when it was really hard to return.

'Why did you?' I asked him that day.

'Perhaps you know the answer. When I hear the national anthem, an electric current goes through me.'

All these years I have reflected, and tried hard to pay attention to the crime from a pacified state. But, each attempt has been a failure. Perhaps this is the most complicated and painful part of the story. My only hope is that I am able to narrate the facts with the precision they demand. The task, I am sadly aware, is nearly impossible. So, let me just focus on the only truth I know...

A week later our class was divided into two groups for factory visits. The chairman accepted my request to join the second, relatively small group. Not Bombay or ONGC, but a two-day visit to factories up north in the mountains; this group was guided and led by Professor Singh. We left on 30 October.

Because I was unwell, my father drove me to the station that day. He insisted on shaking hands with my teacher. Nelly, too, was there on the platform. Although it was the onset of autumn, her light cotton sari exuded the feel of summer. (Her two boys with long hair were at school.) The train was to depart at seven in the morning.

'Is your father an IPS?' Professor Singh took me aside. I remember his soft voice.

Father's uniform made it obvious that he was an elite Indian Police Service officer. However, civilians found it difficult to decode the meaning of stars and ribbons and medals and other signs. Father was a super-cop in Delhi Police, and took orders directly from the Central government.

On 30 October, we visited the pharmaceutical plant in Kasauli (in the colonial times, the building had served as a TB sanatorium). On 31 October, we visited the Mohan Meakin Brewery in the Solan hills (in colonial times, it was called Dyer-Meakin Brewery Dyer was the father of General Dyer who ordered colonial India's most brutal killings of defenseless 'natives', the Amritsar massacre in 1919).

I remember still, the enzymes, the smell of fermentation reactors and the hum of giant crushers, centrifuges, and heat exchangers. Stage-3 washing with excess carbon dioxide to remove harmful gases from the liquid, the Bengali quality control officer (a teetotaler and a Brahmin) who tasted 'the thing' after it 'matured'. Alcohol was pumped like water from a muddy brown river to the bottling zone of the plant. In my ears, I still carry an echo of the strange music the pasteurized glass bottles produced on the conveyor belt. Fifty thousand bottles a day.

During our return journey, Professor Singh regaled us with chemical stories, catalysts, and runaway reactions. Bubbles, drops, and particles ... Professor Singh had a broad smile. To this day, I cannot forget his special smile. The catering-wallah passed by and we ordered twenty-one lunches, eight veg and thirteen non-veg. The veg thalis had daal and chaawal and dahi, and oily parathas with achaar. Non-veg ones had fish curry, or mutton with gravy. I ordered fish and this detail for some reason is stuck. The fish is stuck inside me. Some chootiya mentioned surrogate mothers, and then a bad joke about female mannequins, and Professor Singh stared at our silliness and there was a stunned silence. Then someone suggested antakshari and we sang old film songs, and Michael Jackson, and Prince, and even David Bowie, until someone played the radio, first All India Radio, and immediately afterwards, the short-wave BBC Radio, which confirmed that Mrs Gandhi had been assassinated by her own bodyguards.

Good, a class fellow said, and Professor Singh stood up and raised his voice. You should not talk like this, he scolded the student.

The slow-moving train got more and more delayed, and perhaps it was one of the most difficult nights for the entire country.

Early in the morning, we saw people defecating by the railway tracks, Subzi Mandi passed by, and then the train arrived at the New Delhi station. Even before it came to a complete halt, we saw traces of violence on the platform, but there were cops stationed there, and because the cops were armed with guns and lathis, we thought the situation was under control. We spontaneously formed a circle around Professor Singh (for he was the only Sikh in our group) and stepped out of the bogie.

I wish my father had been there to receive us, then there would have been no need to worry, but in those days cell phones didn't exist.

Suddenly an angry mob, armed with the most elementary weapons (metallic rods and rubber tyres) crossed the railway line and climbed onto the platform. 'Khoon ka badla khoon se'… 'Give us that traitor sardar.' We started to run. 'Blood for blood.' What broke the circle was a vespa scooter on the platform. Sudden screeching of breaks, tyre marks, smell of rubber. A photojournalist in a yellow windcheater started snapping pictures of the mob, which had fished out our professor. 'Stop taking pictures,' said one of the thugs, 'otherwise we kill you.'

'This traitor Sikh is going to take pictures.' The thug pointed at Professor Singh. 'Those who want to save him, we kill you.' He kicks the journalist in the balls, snatches the camera, destroys the roll. I remain paralysed. The thug snatches our professor's suitcase, 'Sardarji, our mother is dead and you are not crying? Cry, behnchod. Gaddaar ke londay, beat your chest.' He unzips the suitcase, rummages through the contents, old and new, pulls out something that looks like a souvenier for Nelly, and a pahari doll (most probably for a child) and a Himachali achkan (most likely for his son). 'Nice wrist watch.'

Then the thug gestures for the other lumpens to go ahead; they spray gasoline from the journalist's scooter on our teacher, slip a rubber tyre around his neck.

'Let me go. What have I done?' I can hear Professor Singh shout. The tyre constrains his arms. 'Sardar, you behenchod, you killed our mother. Gaddaar, now we kill you.'

'Stop it,' I say, 'you can't do this, he is our teacher.'

'Khoon ka badla khoon se'... 'saala sardar ki aulad ... gaddaar ki aulad'. Although it is early morning, his breath stinks of rum.

Half of my class fellows disappear others repeat the same thing over and over, 'This is madness.'

I urge the cops to take immediate action. I tell them that I happen to be the son of the police chief. At this point, the chief lumpen laughs and spits on Professor Singh's face, douses the tyre with more hydrocarbons and strikes a match.

A senior Congress leader, his Nehru-Gandhi khadi clothes fluttering in the wind, is standing close to the Station Master's office on the platform, guiding the mob like the conductor of a big orchestra, 'Khatam kar do sab sardaron ko. Khatam kar do saanp kay bacchon ko'. (Finish off the Sikhs. Finish these children of snakes.)He is not very tall and wears black glasses.

I will never forget that Congresswallah's black glasses. I feel like confronting him, but stand rooted to the platform.

'This is the way to teach the Sikhs a lesson,' says a bystander.

I take a deep breath, the black glasses are gone. The photojournalist is still trembling, they spare his vespa, and we keep hearing the screams. I still hear those screams. I can't hear enough. We couldn't do a thing. I could do nothing. The only thing I was able to save was a shoe, and that too was lost in the commotion that followed.

It was sickening, you had to see the horror to believe the horror, and it was so unreal I almost didn't believe my own sense organs. But the fire and the smoke were so absolutely real, different from the way it is done in the movies. During combustion, I could not use my knowledge of chemistry and physics to extinguish the flames. How fast they engulfed his entire body. I could do nothing. I was a mere onlooker. In the end, all that remained among the ashes, were a few bones and a steel bracelet. Black like a griddle.

My father had sent an official jeep to pick me up from the station and drop me at the engineering campus. Two of my classmates accompanied me.

As the jeep passed Tolstoy Marg, I saw dozens of Sikh bodies on fire. The smell of burning wool and books (*Adi Granth*) and rubber tyres and human flesh… I saw taxis being smashed. And the black cloud of smoke touched the sky. This was our Eiffel Tower. This was our carnival. Our periodic table of hate.

We passed by the church. The bishop was standing by the giant black-painted cast iron gates, preventing the mob from entering the church. Thousands of children, women and men had taken refuge inside.

It was a Thursday. The jeep driver was in tears, he had seen horrible things. The skinny man trembled, he was on the verge of a nervous breakdown. He said he didn't want to come, but it was Sahib's order and his duty. Those days, my parents lived in a mansion on the posh Amrita Shergill Marg (the road named after the 'mother of modern Indian art'), and I lived in the hostel in the engineering campus.

After this, there are lapses in my memory. And moisture in my eyes. There was too much going on. Too many exams. What conversations I had with my fellow classmates, I have little recall.

I do recall though my thoughts brittle and numb, as if deep inside a Zero Kelvin Dewar flask, and then drifting as fast as the speed of light towards Professor Singh's family. Were they safe? The police jeep was still parked outside the hostel. Instead of going into my room, I asked the driver to take me to Professor Singh's residence in Munirka just outside the engineering campus. The driver urged me to check with Sahib first. So I called Father from the hostel common room using a landline. After three attempts and literally begging his junior officer, Father took hold of the receiver.

'What are you doing to stop the madness?'

Incoherently, I told him about the railway platform scene. Father didn't express any shock. Father only said that I must send the driver back. Abruptly, he hung up.

Because the place was not far, I literally ran towards Munirka. There were smouldering ash particles floating around in the air. Punjab Woollens garment store was being eaten up by orange flames, dark and dense clouds ascending. Sikh shops, schools, houses and places of worship were on fire. I tried to help a man who lay on the street, but he was dead near his freshly cut long hair. Near the market, I saw groups of women fleeing with voluminous loot bags. I particularly recall a red-coloured bag. Near the park, I saw a body being torn apart, people playing tug of war with legs on one side and hands on the other side. All along I did not feel unsafe, because one simple rule or law was clear in that hell – all the violence was directed against the Sikh citizens. These were not 'riots', for not a single Hindu was harmed or killed.

Professor Singh's house looked like a scene right out of Coppola's film, *Apocalypse Now*. Brando inside. Heavily guarded. Not by the cops. But by lumpen youths. One of them had a Bombay filmstar haircut. A few other replicas were sitting inside a white Fiat car, drinking. Others near the car held tridents and iron bars and glass bottles. For some unknown reason, the courage that had left me at the railway platform returned.

'Where are you going?'

'My professor's family lives here.'

'They are safe,' said the self-appointed lumpen chief. 'We are guarding them.'

'We the bodyguards.'

I avoided direct eye-contact.

She was either inside or not. Were the boys safe? I had no idea.

'Go see for yourself. Everything okay here.'

There were ten or twenty of them. Or twenty or thirty. It was hard to estimate. All of a sudden I was able to breathe again, and slowly, I tried to walk.

The jacarandas and bougainvillea stared at me and so did the Semal tree, as I knocked several times and announced my name. Several times.

All the doors were locked. The windows were all curtained.

'Go home.'

It was Nelly's voice. Choked a bit.

'It is me.'

'I know. Go back to your hostel. Right away.'

She didn't ask about Professor Singh. I was the one who knew the exact details about what really had happened to him. She, it was clear then, didn't want to talk.

Realising this, I turned as if all that mattered in the world was to obey her voice. Soon my feet started dragging me towards my room in the engineering hostel.

'Told you they are alright,' the goons laughed.

Most of them had alcohol in them. And they were getting louder by the minute. Nothing about these guards was reassuring. They inspired little confidence. It was certain Nelly and the kids were not safe.

The cops were missing. I did see two or three men in khaki, mingling with the lumpens, but really, it was hard to tell who was a cop and who a lumpen. Then the filmstar haircut stared at me piercingly.

Perhaps that is why I returned.

Back to Nelly.

Once again no resistance was offered.

I knocked again. Several times.

'Nelly, please open.'

She didn't wait long this time. I heard near-instant movement inside. 'Please, Nelly, shall I ask my father to rescue you from here.' The fact is that I had lost all hope of getting help from Father. But this way I knew there was a possibility of getting a response from her, and she did respond.

I heard her walk close to the door. She didn't unlock. Again, she begged me to go home.

Unable to tear myself away from the house, I felt completely helpless.

'Don't worry,' she said.

'What do you mean? Don't worry?'

Don't worry, she says.

This is the situation. The chief lumpen is staring at me all over again. Threatening my body to leave. I ignore him and his buddies, the men in khaki and bright unmourning primary colours. My feet for some unknown reason drag me around the house. The mob on the other side, close to the kitchen, is as big as the mob on this side and both sides are getting noisier and noisier. I tap on the kitchen window.

And stand there waiting.

I knew she would return.

Finally, a hand swishes open the curtain made of beads.

'Don't worry,' she says. Her face looks like a phase-diagram plotted between fear and shame.

'I have already done what the men asked me to do,' she explains.

'You did not.' On their own, her two boys, the twins, appeared close to the window.

At first, I do not recognise them. The boys have no maroon patkas on. Their long, curly hair is freshly cut. Hurriedly, brutally cut. It shows.

'I have already done what the men asked me to do. Now go home,' she repeats. 'We are safe.'

The Morning After

Mridula Garg

DOWNSTAIRS, THEY WERE SHOUTING AGAIN. The Bansals. Her landlord's family. They were forever shouting. If someone were to ask her to describe Delhi in one word, she would say, 'Noise.' Noise that assaulted your senses from all directions at all times. A constant uproar made up of meaningless sounds that you had to suffer, shut up in a small room closed on all sides by other rooms full of noise. Thirty-seven years it had been since she first took refuge in this city and she still had not got used to the noise. No, she was being unfair. Khairpur in Punjab had been no less noisy. But she had the advantage of space there. A medium-sized cottage with a small garden outside. They had grown fruits and vegetables there, even flowers occasionally. They had been the prosperous ones there.

Why remember it now? That was before Partition, before they had turned into faceless refugees. Delhi had given them refuge; she should be grateful, and she was. Only she wished the Bansals were less voluble, or less loud. At least sometimes, they could be silent, could they not, now, at least for a little while, when they received such shattering news? The prime minister,

Indira Gandhi, had been shot, killed by her own bodyguards! It was not two hours since the transistor had announced it. She had been struck dumb. Her sons, Ashok and Ajay, and their friend Sarabjit were there with her in her little room but no one had a word to say. They had been sitting quietly for the last two hours. But not the Bansals.

'Sattoji! Satto Aunty!' There they went again. Good God, it was her name they were calling, father and son together. Now what? Shanti-shanti, she intoned, Om shanti-shanti, as she came out on the little balcony outside her room.

'Keep your sons home,' Bansalji said as soon as he saw her. 'There's a riot on in the city.'

'Saw four Sikhs being cut to pieces myself,' his son Manku added.

'Sikhs? Why Sikhs?'

'She was killed by Sikhs.'

'By her guards, the radio said.'

'Yes, yes, they were Sikhs.'

'So what?' Ashok was at her side questioning them. Out of the corner of her eye, she saw Sarabjit come out of the room with Ajay. In a flash she had turned around, sending Sarabjit to the inside wall of the room with a violent push. At the same time, she shouted loudly for Ashok, startling him into coming in. Quickly, she bolted the door from inside and stood panting before them.

'What's wrong?' the boys asked at the same time.

Moving close to them, she whispered. 'No one is to go out and no one is to know he is here.'

The three of them burst out laughing. She shut up Sarabjit immediately by placing her hand over his mouth. 'Silence. Not a sound,' she hissed.

'You've gone mad!' Ashok sounded angry.

'You heard. There's a riot in the city. People are killing Sikhs.'

'Crazy, Ma, you know the Delhiwalas are born rumourmongers.'

'With solid lung power.' Sarabjit had removed her hand from his mouth and was chuckling with the rest.

'Let's go see.' Ajay turned to the door but she was there blocking it like a wall.

'Sarabjit is in danger. We must hide him,' she whispered.

'What danger?' Sarabjit interjected. 'Everyone knows me here.'

'That's the danger. Everyone knew Papa in 1947. He was the station master in Khairpur. That's how... but I am wasting my time. Come with me.' She took him by the hand and pushed him into the store. 'Sit here and don't put on the light. Open only when I knock three times like this.' She demonstrated.

'Some detective story you have been reading. Okay, I'll sit here. But what if I suffocate, Auntyji?'

'You won't. The skylight is there.' She showed him the small hole in the outer wall that opened into the back lane. She was about to close the door when he held her hand. 'Will you starve me then, my dear Aunty?' he said and laughed.

She did not. With utmost seriousness, she put a few chapattis and some vegetables on a plate and handed it to him along with a bottle of water. After closing the door, she locked it and turned to face her scowling sons.

'What is all this in aid of?' uttered a bitter Ashok.

'You were not there in 1947. I was. I know,' she said.

'That was different. The country had been partitioned. Why will people kill each other now? They are not mad.'

'They go mad.'

'All of them.'

'No, some.'

'Silly.'

'It is not. One lighted match is all it needs to ignite a dump of charcoal. Once a crowd gathers, it soon becomes a mob. A mob out to celebrate or annihilate. A man in a mob is not a man.'

'Which book is that from?' Ashok teased but before she could answer, Ajay interjected.

'But where do they come from?'

Where did they come from, the rioters and the killers? Until yesterday, everyone was busy earning his bread, no one had time for anyone else. How could they suddenly come to know each other so intimately today to form cohesive groups, with separate identities, organised to kill each other? Who were those people, where did they come from, and where did they hide again once it was over?

'Where do they come from, Ma?' Ajay repeated his question.

'No one is coming from anywhere,' Ashok cut in. 'Ma's got 1947 on her mind.'

'Sattoji!' Her name rang through, bringing her to the balcony before it could be repeated. Bansal again.

'Is Ashok at home?'

'Yes.'

'And his friend... that Sikh fellow?'

'He left right after you did, at three, after the news.'

'Don't let him in if he comes back.'

'Never. Who can trust them now?' she said bitterly.

'And why not?' Ashok butted in. 'Have you no shame, Ma?'

'Shut up.'

'They were there, all around the medical institute, distributing sweets, dancing the bhangra, while the poor lady lay dead. Won't the Hindus want to kill? Have they no blood coursing in their veins?'

'You saw them dancing and eating sweets?' asked a baffled Ashok.

'Am I lying then?'

'You saw... did you really?' Ashok's voice grew shaky.

'There is no other way to teach them a lesson. They have been killing Hindus for so long in Punjab, we did nothing...'

'Why didn't you? If you had gone there to take revenge, that would have been something. What's the fun in killing innocent Sikhs here?'

'Why are you so eager to defend the enemy? This is self-defense, son. If we don't kill them now, they'll run over the whole country tomorrow. Am I wrong, Sattoji?'

'No, absolutely right,' she said in a strong voice.

'You think so... truly you do? I don't. You hear me, I won't.' Ashok cried out as if in pain.

'No point hiding under your Ma's pallu, son, come out and see for yourself, if you dare.' Bansal laughed at his face.

'I will.' He shoved her roughly aside and ran down the stairs into the street.

She went back into the room and began a chant of prayer to Bajrangbali, the great monkey god Hanuman, the protector of the weak and the young. Bajrangbali, look after him, protect my son, she intoned again, and again, Bajrangbali, Bajrangbali, Bajrangbali...

Inside the store, Sarabjit heard them and froze in terror. He was about to put a piece of chapatti into his mouth when he heard Satto Aunty say, 'Who can trust them now?' What about him? He had put himself completely in their hands and they were plotting his… He let the chapatti fall and went to the door. There was a gap between the door and the floor, where a thin stream of light filtered in from the room. By now he had got used to seeing in that dim light. He examined the door thoroughly. There was no bolt inside! The door was bolted or locked from outside. He could not protect himself by bolting it from his side. When they decided to open it, they would have him at their mercy, alone, unarmed, with his back to the wall. He went over the cage-like room with his hands, inch by inch, searching for something that could be used as a weapon. All he found was a board of wood. He clung to it with both hands, ready to strike at the first sound.

It was the first quarter of the evening when even Delhi fell into an uneasy silence. The daytime cacophony died down, albeit slowly and with spasmodic grunts and growls. This happened every night. Only this time Satto did not welcome the silence; she left the radio on to keep her company in her lonely vigil. She found it soothing with its mournful rendition of religious songs and tunes appropriate to the passing on of a leader. It brought her own sorrow back to her; it was but seven years that her husband had died. With him had died her dream of living in the other Delhi, the Delhi of green parks and wide roads. The Delhi of the tourist brochures, the beautiful capital of a lovely country. Delhi of the movies and television, that's what she had always called it. It was only in the movies and later on the TV in the Bansals' house that she had ever seen that Delhi, the one that boasted of being a garden city, where the rich had huge one-storey bungalows filled with colourful flowers in the winter seasons and coolers and air-conditioners in the summer. Not only were there gardens inside the houses, but the traffic islands also erupted in a blaze of colour with the advent of winter. Then there were the huge, well-tended public parks, which reminded her of her native town in Punjab, each of them as big as the whole town. But it had not the wide and smooth roads of Delhi, on which the cars of the rich ran merrily, unmindful of traffic regulations or the less fortunate ones who went about on foot. Why, in that Delhi of movie sets, there were even fountains spouting water at the height of summer, when the tap in her house did not yield the thinnest trickle of water. The likes of her had to depend on the municipal tanker for their minimum needs.

That was her Delhi, this motley jumble of closely built small tenements amid narrow lanes and alleys in Sadar Bazaar, a part of Old Delhi, as they used to call it once. They had stopped doing that for some time now; why, she did not know. All she knew was that there was a newer Delhi that was even better than New Delhi and it lay in the southern part of the city. She knew it, thanks to the TV at the Bansals. She caught a glimpse of the spacious flower-carpeted city each time a foreign dignitary came to visit and did a round of the capital. They always saw the tour on the box, and in colour too. The Bansals had plenty of money, what with their hardware shop and rooms to let. Not that she meant to be ungrateful. They were not bad people, never threatened her with evictions or demands for higher rent like so many landlords she had heard of. Those people knew how to twist the arm of the law, tenant protection or no tenant protection, and she a widow with two young sons... But not the Bansals. How nicely they invited her to come and watch TV at their place, the Sunday feature film, the cricket matches, everything. The only thing she had never gone to see was the Republic Day parade—not that they did not ask her, but she wanted to retain the memory of the parade she had seen live at India Gate as it was. Her husband had taken her there, had purchased the most expensive tickets—well, almost. That was the only time she had seen the Delhi of the movies and television in real life. Indira Gandhi had been the prime minister then and now she was dead. Killed! Om shanti-shanti-shanti.

May her soul rest in peace. Peace was the most important thing, not money or comfort. It was true that she, Satto, had to sell a small plot of land her husband had managed to buy in the southern part of Delhi, then a patch of wilderness but well on its way to prosperous development now, or so she had heard. She had to sell because she had no money to build even one room and the municipal authorities were not willing to let the land lie waste. Destiny, who could fight it. She was better than millions of others. She had a permanent job as a teacher of domestic science in a government school close by. She earned her living and lived in an independent room with a store and even a small, very small, balcony to breathe in fresh air. Ah, she was a lucky one.

The silence grew more palpable. The dogs had stopped barking, she realised. The bhajans from the radio filled the silence of the room with their sweet sound and her with peace. May her soul rest in peace, she murmured again. May all their souls rest in peace. Yes, peace was what was most important. That was what her mother always said when they first came as refugees to Delhi. Satto, pray that never again may anyone lose his loved ones in a riot, pray that all souls rest in peace so that no one roams around inciting people to hatred and violence. Om shanti-shanti-shanti.

Filled with peace, she got up, went to the kitchen and called Ajay to come and eat.

'Are you going to keep Sarabjit in the store all night?' he asked.

Suddenly she laughed and said, 'I'm a crazy fool, am I not, to worry so, shutting the poor child in the store to lull my own wild fears. Let me go unlock him.'

She got up to hear a long, drawn-out human scream rent the air. Petrified, she turned to Ajay and asked, 'Did you hear it too?'

She did not give him time to answer. Cautioning him to silence, she raised the volume of the radio, then went to work with furious but hushed speed. Motioning for Ajay to help, she moved the old, high-domed almirah that stood in one corner of the room to block the entrance to the store. Fortunately, it blocked off the door completely. No one could know at first glance that there was a door to another room there. Carefully, she changed the position of the bed, the wooden box and the chairs to make the room look properly laid out. They had to use all their strength to ensure nothing dragged on the floor; the slightest sound could make the Bansals suspicious. She did not forget to wipe out the dust marks with a wet cloth. She could not possibly use a broom at that hour after sunset; they would immediately know and wonder at her doing something so inauspicious with the poor lady not yet consigned to the flames.

And Ashok... where was Ashok? Why had he not returned home yet? Her heart cried out, sick with worry for her son as she prepared to protect the other one. Bajrangbali, look after my son, bring him back home soon. You know the murky narrow bylanes of Sadar Bazaar are no place for a young boy to be out at night. You know what crimes are committed there in the dark.

Make him come back, Bajrangbali, take care of him tonight of all the dark, terrifying nights.

Inside the store, it suddenly grew pitch dark. The thin pencil of light disappeared. Fools! Why did they have to put out the light in the room? Didn't they know that this would put him in total darkness? He knelt down to peer under the door and was surprised to find a wall blocking his view. Now what! How could the wall shrink to come so close to the door? Waheguru, he prayed, was his brain getting addled in this airless room? He shook himself. No, he must not imagine things. He remembered Satto Aunty telling him not to put on the light. So there was a light inside. See, no need to panic. He was going to put it on once just to see.

He groped all the walls looking for a switch. Nothing. No way to put on the light from inside. So she had lied to him! Oh God!

He did not expect this of Ashok's mother. For five years, he had come to their house and been treated like a son. Ashok and he had been through school and college together; they were even now planning to be partners in a scooter repair shop, with the mother pitching in with funds. And now this!

Was it his fault that Indira Gandhi had been killed by her Sikh guards? Why did they kill her, the bastards? Had they not vowed to protect her, eaten her salt, been chosen to guard her? Then they had gone and shot her, sixteen times, a woman and unarmed. That was not like a true Sikh warrior, a Khalsa. Why, we do not even hit an animal twice. If it is beheaded the first time, fine; otherwise, the meat is taboo for us. Who knows—the Hindus might have killed her themselves, grown hair and beards to do it. To let the Sikhs suffer! They were quite capable of it. Our people might be hot-headed, but not cheats. Traitors never.

Then why am I hiding here like a coward? Are not my hands and feet enough to break the door open and confront Ashok's mother? I don't wish her ill; I'll tell her she has been taken for a ride by them, the eunuchs. It is not right to heed strangers and reject your own; am I not like your own son?

Suddenly, the store was filled with a red glow: flashes of light that blinded him for a moment, then a red afterglow. Where had he seen it before? Yes, he remembered, it rose out of the funeral pyre of his father, which he had lighted himself only last year. There were red glints like this all over the crematorium, so many pyres there had been that day. I suppose that is how it is every day here, he thought. Today... But the crematorium was miles away; how was the glow shining in this room? 'Waheguru, help me, this is a fire!'

He could see angry red flames streaking the sky from the skylight. 'It's in this neighbourhood, behind this very house. Waheguru, it is this house which is on fire! Have they all gone, leaving me here to be burned alive? Motherfuckers! You don't know me, I'm a Khalsa, equal to a hundred thousand of you. I'll not die trapped like a rat. I'll kick the door and be out to take revenge. I'll kill you all before I die. *Jo bole so nihal, sat sri akal*! I'm ready to die for the faith. So help me God!'

Satto felt the kick on the door vibrate through the spine. What was the boy up to? Did he want the whole neighbourhood there? Should she go into the store and see, remove the almirah and... She was still undecided when she heard the footsteps on the stairs. They were on their way up! She ran out of the room to collide with Manku on the top step.

'The Sikhs have attacked!' Both father and son shouted together. 'They are firing from inside the gurudwara.'

'Ashok,' she muttered.

'Has he come back?'

She shook her head.

'Why did you let him go? Didn't we warn you? The Sikhs cannot be trusted. Look at the fire outside.'

Meanwhile, Ajay had run out on the balcony. He came back and said, 'What have the Sikhs to do with the fire? It's the gurudwara which is on fire.'

The gurudwara! On fire! The house of God! Mercy! She had gone so often to the gurudwara in the past to listen to the gurbani, the readings of sacred texts, which both Sikhs and Hindus attended. So what if she was a Hindu in the gurudwara, the house of worship of the Sikhs. Had they not always lived like brothers of one faith in this city? The Guru was their teacher too, their ladder to God. Mercy. Forgive them, O Lord. Protect my son. 'Ashok,' she muttered faintly.

'So the gurudwara is on fire, eh? What did you expect? If they fire on us, won't we hit back?' Manku had his hand on Ajay's collar.

'Ashok… what about Ashok?' she started wailing.

It had its effect. Manku turned to her and said, 'I'll go and look for him. Come with me.' He took Ajay by the hand and clattered down the stairs.

'Bansalji, my son,' she was weeping in right earnest now.

'Don't worry, Sattoji, Manku will find him and bring him home. Has he gone?'

'Who?' her voice shook.

'That friend of Ashok's?'

Sarabjit had held back after that one powerful kick on the door. He could hear the shouts and accusations of the Bansals clearly. He stood close to the door with the wooden board clasped firmly in his hand and waited for the woman to answer the question Bansal had asked her.

Despite straining his ears to the maximum, he could not catch her answer. Why was that woman speaking in such low tones? The Bansals were shouting loudly enough. Waheguru, what plot were they hatching against him? This was not the time to run out; the house was not on fire. It was the gurudwara... Curse the bastards, they had destroyed the house of God. But he must wait, catch the woman alone.

On the other side of the door, Bansal repeated in a menacing tone, 'Has he gone or not?'

'Long ago,' she said amid sobs, so softly that Bansal could hardly hear her. 'It must be all over with him by now. But Ashok...'

'I'll go see,' Bansal went down.

She flung herself on the cot in the room and started praying to Hanuman, the protector of the weak and the young.

Sarabjit stood alert, clinging to the door with his body and to the wooden board with his hands. There was just this door between him and death. He was ready. If he had to die, he had to. But he would die like a true Khalsa, after killing the enemy.

The night claims its own, however sharp the blades of fire. A time came when both Sarabjit, clinging to the door, and Satto, moaning her prayers on the cot, fell into an uneasy sleep.

Each night has a dawn. Only some are darker than the night before. Such was the first morning of November, which marked the end of the night of 31 October 1984.

He entered his own house like a thief, tapped on the door as if the slightest noise would bring the house down. A single tap was enough for Satto to be up and at the door. She opened it only after ascertaining who it was in a muted whisper and just wide enough to admit him.

She looked at him aghast. Her husband had returned from the dead! But how? Had she not seen him consigned to the flames and reduced to ashes with her own eyes? She was there when her young sons had collected the remains of the charred bones from the crematorium and taken them to their final resting place in the river Ganga at Haridwar. He had grown old in his youth with the sadness that had wasted him, but he had found rest in death. Not once had he come to haunt her in the past seven years. Why now?

He firmly held her hand with his and bolted the door with the other. 'He can't be kept here, Ma,' he said.

Ma! She stared at him and realised with a shock that he was not the ghost of her dead husband but her younger son, Ajay. But what had happened to his face? How could he go from fourteen to forty in one night?

'What...what...?' she fumbled.

'It was a blunder. I went to the police station last night.'

'Then?'

'I asked them to help Sarabjit. They said to me, "You call yourself a Hindu!We would help you if you had come to us after killing him."'

'What will we do?' Satto cried.

'We'll have to cut his hair.'

'He'll never agree.'

'He will. I'll tell him all that I saw last night,' he said in a cold dry tone.

Was he the same boy who had asked her last night, 'But where do they come from?'

'Hurry. We must have him out.'

'Why, what's the danger here?' she asked and got the answer immediately. From both sides of the street rose a crescendo of slogans. 'Kill! Kill! Kill! the enemies of the nation!'

Ajay pulled her behind the almirah. She opened the door of the store and went inside.

Sarabjit had woken with a start at the mad din in the street to find that the wooden board had slipped from his hands. The woman was upon him before he could find it. He clenched his fists and raised them to bash her on the head. But she was quicker. She had him in a tight embrace before he could move.

'Son! My child! Hurry! Let Ajay cut your hair and take you with him.' She was sobbing.

Ajay was there too, with scissors and a razor ready in his hands. Sarabjit stood frozen with his hands raised above his head. Outside, the slogans were punctuated by tortured cries of pain.

They heard a truck and a few motorbikes rattle past, and then the house opposite theirs was on fire. And the cries. God, those fearsome cries of human agony. Yet, they were pruning his hair like high-powered machines. Satto made him wear Ashok's well-worn shirt and trousers before Ajay finished the shave. The neighbours had seen the clothes so often, they were sure to mistake him for Ashok; both Sarabjit and Ashok were the same height and build.

But Ashok—where was Ashok? Her heart cried out but there was no time for thoughts of anyone but Sarabjit. He tried to thank her, to say goodbye, but there was no time for that either.

'Quick.' Ajay was hustling him. 'The mob's enjoying the fire. Let's get the bike. You sit at the back.'

That was right; that way the crowd would see more of Ajay's face than Sarabjit's.

The Bansals were standing on the rooftop to enjoy the tamasha. Sarabjit and Ajay got out of the house and managed to reach the road without being accosted. Satto locked the store and pulled the almirah back before it. She stood there with a silent prayer on her lips, afraid to go out and look, yet drawn to the balcony by the wild hunting cries of the crowd.

Could one call it a crowd, or was it a stampede of wild animals turned into men or men turned into rapacious beasts? Were the boys out on a jihad or a jashna? There was nothing but the fever of the chase. There had been an assassination then also, in 1948, of another Gandhi; people had come out of their homes in droves to gather in the streets. But that was a crowd of mourners gathered there by common consent in self-condemnation and a will to expiate. No kitchen fires had burned that night and the morning after. This morning the houses themselves were afire in a murderous aftermath.

She stood transfixed on the balcony and wondered what she was witnessing: a mourning gone berserk or a celebration of a windfall of violence? A jashan, maybe a jihad, but on no account a demonstration of grief, no, not that, ever.

With a prayer on her lips, she scanned the crowd below, and saw that Ajay and Sarabjit had not yet reached the safe precincts beyond the frenzied mob. Bajrangbali-Guru Kirpal, help them, she called out to both the protectors together and leaned a little further to keep them in sight. She was appalled to see four young men drag an old, white-bearded Sikh on the road right in front of her house.

'Let the old man go, you beasts,' she screamed but to no avail. She was about to run down when she realised she still had Sarabjit's long hair in her hand. Before she could decide what to do with it, a white car came to a stop in front of her house and a man looked out with a smug smile. Why, he was the man she had voted for in the last elections. So had her Sikh neighbours. But she didn't have the time to shudder or recoil, for the man was out of the car, shouting like a hunter with a buck in sight.

'Stop. Stop the shaved Sikhrda on the bike.'

'No!' she held the hair aloft. 'I have him inside the house. See. See the hair. I cut them to lure him into the store. I have him locked in. Come and get him. Those are my sons on the bike. Come quickly, he must not escape.'

She was like the bloodthirsty goddess Kali seeking the destruction of evil. The tongues of fire touched the visage of the goddess with an awesome allure. The long black tresses swung back and forth in rhythm to the dance of the flames, inviting the faithful to keep in step. The crowd ran up, like a pack of wolves with their tongues dangling out, smelling blood.

'There,' she said and pointed to the almirah in front of the store. It did not take bare hands more than a moment to wrest the locked doors apart. They growled at the stuff packed inside and turned to tear her apart. She was still in control. 'Behind it, inside the store,' she said firmly.

They pulled the almirah away with all its weight as if it contained nothing but feathers. Then they wrenched the lock off the door as if it was not there. They were in and out of the store and upon her almost in the same instant.

'Lies! Hand him over or...'

'You call yourselves Hindus? You shameless brutes, is this what your religion has taught you?' she said evenly, framed by the fire and the dark tresses. 'What if it was your son Manku being burnt alive? Or trampled to death? You have sons and daughters too. Have mercy, my brothers, if you want mercy for your children.' She folded her hands and the hair formed a shield. 'Come with me, brothers, let us go and save the old Sardarji. Come.' She pressed against the railing and started to point at the old man being kicked and beaten on the road, but stopped, petrified.

She would have flung herself down as all composure deserted her, had not an iron rod landed on her head. Her skull broke open. Sarabjit's hair was splattered with Satto's blood. 'Ashok...' she managed to mumble as darkness engulfed her. She had seen her elder son on the outer fringe of the murderous crowd on the road.

Trilokpuri

Vikram Kapur

MOHAMMAD WOKE UP THAT MORNING to a knot in his stomach. Not the kind of knot that accrues from worry or fear—it was far too loose for that. It was more like an uneasiness that had planted itself in his gut and kept prodding him as if to say I'm here. He wondered what had brought it on. There was nothing pressing about the day. It was a Saturday. He didn't have to go to Delhi University where he was a professor of media studies. His wife Razia had landed safely in Hyderabad last night to present a paper at an academic conference. (She taught English literature at Jamia.) When they spoke over the phone last night, she was upbeat and looking forward to the presentation, which was today. Her text that had beeped in to his cell phone earlier that morning communicated more of the same. What was more, just two days ago, Razia's gynaecologist had eased his biggest concern by informing them that Razia's pregnancy was going fine with both mother and child doing well.

Then why was he feeling this way?

Clad in a blue kurta-pyjama, he sat on the edge of his bed with his narrow chin propped on clasped hands. He was a slim man of forty-five with skin the colour of sapodilla. He had a full head of wiry black hair. His round glasses had a penchant for sliding down the bridge of his long, pointed nose, prompting his small hands to leap up in a bid to restore them. Over the years, that action had become so ingrained that his hands felt obliged to meddle with his glasses at regular intervals, irrespective of whether they were sliding down his nose or not. Tiny lines poked out of his eyebrows and the corners of his mouth. Right now those lines were more deeply etched than usual as he attempted to unravel the mystery of the knot with his lips clamped together. Only the doorbell announcing the arrival of the cleaning lady pulled him away from his musing.

The confounded knot proved to be maddeningly resilient, beating back even the antacid he took in his bid to untie it. As the morning dwindled, a frown darkened Mohammad's forehead. He was no longer intrigued by the knot; he was exasperated. Its continuing presence was a blemish on the otherwise unsullied horizon of his day. Round mid-day, he made up his mind to go get a coffee at his neighbourhood café. Maybe going out was what he needed to disentangle himself from the annoying knot.

His flat was on the second floor of a three-storey building. Dressed in dark trousers and an open-necked check shirt, he walked carefully down a dusty staircase that wound into a small, uncarpeted lobby. The lobby was empty at the moment. He exited it through a brightly painted brown door to encounter Abhay, who lived downstairs, and his six-year-old son.

Abhay was ten years younger than him and almost as tall. The slouch in his shoulders, though, made him appear much shorter. He had lost most of his hair and what was left clustered in a black clump towards the back of his head. He had a genial ruddy face and a paunch that drooped like a sagging breast inside his white t-shirt. The t-shirt dangled loosely over a pair of yellow bermuda shorts. On his feet, he was wearing leather sandals. Like Mohammad he wore glasses, albeit with thicker lenses. His pudgy hands were full of bags of chips and plastic bottles of Coca Cola. He waved a bulging bag of Lays by way of greeting. The boy smiled and said, 'Good morning, Uncle.' This could be my son in a few years. The thought made Mohammad forget about his stomach and a smile spread effortlessly across his face.

'Just went out to get some supplies for the game,' Abhay said.

The 2011 Cricket World Cup final between India and Sri Lanka was going to be played in Mumbai that afternoon. The knot had squeezed any thought of it out of Mohammad's mind.

'If you don't have any other plans, why don't you come and watch it with us?' Abhay continued.

Abhay was being neighbourly, inviting him over for the game. He had to know that Mohammad was alone that day; after all, they employed the same cleaning lady.

Mohammad had always felt diffident around Abhay. When they met for the first time, soon after Abhay moved into the building six months ago, Abhay barely gave him a chance to talk. First, he went on about Rahim, a friend from school, then about Tahir and Imran, two friends from the accountancy firm where he worked, and then Ahmad, a friend who lived in Mumbai... Are all your friends Muslims? Mohammad was tempted to ask. Surely you know a few Hindus, maybe even a Christian, a Parsi or a Jew?

In Mohammad's experience, the typical Hindu came in two shades. One who believed that every Muslim was an angry man with a beard and a gun and made no bones about it, and the other who flaunted his liberal stripes no matter what he believed. Abhay oozed the second type.

He said he'd see if he could make it before saying goodbye. To his relief, Abhay didn't press him. Mohammad checked the mailbox, next to the front gate, on his way out and found a letter addressed to him with no return address on the back of the envelope. He tucked it away in his trousers pockets. He'd read it at the café.

His car was parked under a peepal tree in front of the building. A large gate, with an iron grill, loomed on the other side of the street. Such gates had first risen to separate well-to-do neighbourhoods from the rest of Delhi. Now they were cordoning off sections of neighbourhoods. The boundary walls of the homes to his right and left had inched higher over the years, with several homes crouching behind thick trees as if trying to hide. Where there had once been houses there were now compounds with blocks of flats. With far too many residents packed inside each flat building, the nameplates next to the front gate merely displayed the street address or the name of the property.

Mohammad had first encountered something like that in the wake of the anti-Sikh riots of 1984, where rich Sikhs rubbed out their own names from outside their homes to replace them with names like Krishna Villa and Lakshmi Niwas. The whole practice had reminded him of Muslim actors in Bollywood taking on Hindu names after Partition.

It took him a few minutes to reach the market. Evading a stray cow, he eased into a parking slot on a dusty patch next to the road. A diminutive parking attendant handed him a pink ticket that he stashed in his pockets. A line of stalls huddled next to the broken steps leading into the shopping complex. There was a juice stall, a chai stall, a book stall and a stall for buying cigarettes and paan. Mohammad went up the steps carefully to walk over the cracked concrete slabs in the direction of the cafe. Brightly painted signs grinned all around him—Nike, Adidas, Benneton, Casio, Pizza Hut. A legless beggar, hunched on a low platform with wooden wheels, thrust out a hand. Mohammad looked away. When he heard the cart creak behind him, he practically ran to get on the other side of the café's glass door. Glancing over his shoulder, he saw that the beggar hadn't moved from his spot.

The café had an orange and brown interior, with tables and chairs the colour of golden raisin. The pastries nestled in a glass case next to the counter. A coffeemaker slurped in the back. The place was empty, except for two white tourists poring over a city map. A barista, in an orange uniform, came to take Mohammad's order. The TV, attached to the wall in the corner, was playing a news channel with the volume turned down. Two cricket pundits were discussing India's chances in the final that afternoon. Mohammad recalled watching the semi-final against Pakistan in his office. Two new executive assistants had exchanged glances after he clapped for a textbook straight drive by a Pakistani batsman. He wondered if the same would happen if he cheered one of the Sri Lankans today.

He opened the letter to catch his breath as he read the first line: *Now that you would be a father yourself you'd know how I've felt all these years...*

The letter was from Mr Bawa. Mr Bawa didn't know that he had no kids; that only now, after twelve years of marriage, Razia had got pregnant. His letter hearkened back to 1984, where Mohammad gave up on his dream of becoming a Bollywood lyricist and moved to Delhi to pursue a degree in media studies. It was around the time Prime Minister Indira Gandhi was assassinated by two Sikh bodyguards. Jeet Bawa, a former Sikh classmate from school in Chandigarh, was a student at Delhi University. That day Jeet was helping him move into a flat he had rented in Trilokpuri. By the time they learnt of the assassination and the anti-Sikh riots it sparked, it was too late. Before Jeet could get out of the neighbourhood, he was waylaid by a bunch of goons and beaten up. Later, he succumbed to his injuries.

The last time Mohammad saw Mr Bawa was when he came from Chandigarh to collect Jeet's battered body. The slack jaw and glassy eyes floated in front of him. Swallowing, he put down the letter.

They had finished emptying half the packing cases when they learnt about the assassination… from one of Mohammad's neighbours coming home early in case trouble ensued. Jeet said he'd better go. He wanted to get back to his hostel as soon as possible. His family back in Chandigarh would be sick with worry. There wasn't even a phone in the flat for him to call them.

After Jeet had left, Mohammad wondered whether he should have told him to shave or at least cut his hair. He had quelled the thought, thinking Jeet might get offended. But maybe he should have spoken up.

He started as someone began pounding his front door. A shrill voice called out his name. 'I'm coming,' he yelled, and stepped as fast as he could around the packing cases scattered in the living room on his way to the door. His neighbour's twelve-year-old son stood panting outside.

'Kya paagal ho gaye ho, you're trying to break my door down?' he admonished the boy.

'Uncle, aapka Sikh friend. . . .' The boy paused to catch his breath. Mohammad's mouth went dry. He grabbed the boy's shoulders. 'What happened?'

'I just saw four men beating him.'

'What?'

'Yes, Uncle. It was on the dirt track that leads to the main road. I...'

He was already running. Down the stairs and out into the alley. The sun crouching low on yellow flat blocks. A warren of lanes. Stinking open drains. Catching elbows and forearms. A volley of curses. His slippers scratching dust. His breath spilling out in gasps.

Upon reaching the dirt track, he halted, gulping down air. Pain pulsed in his side. A few men were clustered in a circle. Wiping the sweat from his eyes, he pushed his way to the centre of the cluster.

'Haye Allah!' His hands leaped to his head.

Jeet lay on the ground in a bloody heap.

'Jeet,' he said, kneeling down.

There was no answer. He shook him by the shoulder. There was still no answer. To his relief, he made out a throb in Jeet's pulse. He asked if anyone knew a doctor. One of the men said a nursing orderly named Ram Janak lived nearby. Ram Janak worked the night shift. So he'd be home at the moment. Help me take him there, Mohammad said. It was better than leaving him on the dirt track.

Ram Janak turned out to be a short greying man in his fifties. When he saw that Jeet was a Sikh, he tried to shut the door. What kind of nursing orderly turns away a badly injured man, Mohammad demanded. Ram Janak set his lips together. But he opened the door. They lay Jeet down on a rope bed in one of the rooms. Ram Janak went to call an ambulance, only to find that his phone was dead.

He was taken aback; he had been talking on it only a few

minutes before they arrived. Mohammad asked Ram Janak whether any one of his neighbours had a phone. Ram Janak shook his head. The nearest phone was in a flat in the next building. Mohammad said he'd go there and make the call.

The phone in the adjacent building was dead as well. Its owner sent him to a flat in a building hundred yards away. That phone was also dead.

Mohammad decided to return to Ram Janak's flat. He wanted to see how Jeet was getting on. Then he'd go to the main road and use a pay phone. There was something wrong with the telephone lines in the neighbourhood.

He hadn't gone far before he was confronted by a middle-aged man in a white kurta-pyjama. He recognised him as a local Congress neta. The neta had several men with him, including a police constable in full uniform. The men were carrying machetes, lathis, hockey sticks and cans of kerosene oil.

'Who are you?' the neta demanded.

'I live here,' Mohammad answered in the best voice he could summon.

'I asked who you are – Hindu, Muslim, Sikh?'

A man with a lathi, standing next to the neta, was licking his lips. Fear rippled through Mohammad. 'Muslim,' he mumbled.

'The bastard is lying,' the man with the lathi cried out. 'He's a Sikh.'

Mohammad's chest constricted. "How can I be a Sikh? Just look at me,' he said in a tremulous voice.

'Today those chootias are cutting their hair and shaving their beards,' the man shot back.

'Well, that won't save the maaderchods,' someone shouted from the back. 'Now that we have cut the telephone wires they can't even call out.'

Mohammad's mouth felt as if he had swallowed sawdust. He held up his right wrist, 'See, I'm not even wearing a kara,' he said.

'You could have taken it off,' the neta said.

The man with the lathi was grinning. The grin reminded Mohammad of a wolf baring his teeth. His heart was hammering inside his chest as if it wanted to get out. Quickly, he unbuttoned his trousers and let them fall. Dropping his underwear, he showed his penis which was clearly circumcised.

'Alright, I believe you,' the neta said.

He glanced at the sheet of paper in his hands. 'There should be a Sikh family in the next gali. Come on.'

They set off like a pack of attack dogs. Mohammad waited until they were out of sight, before running to Ram Janak's flat as fast as he could. 'We've got to get him out of here,' he started the moment Ram Janak opened the front door.

Ram Janak's drawn face made him pause. Mohammad gazed disbelievingly at him. It couldn't be.

Slowly, Ram Janak shook his head.

Now Mr Bawa had sent a letter, almost twenty-seven years later. Jeet's younger brother, Joginder, a human rights lawyer, had spent a lifetime trying to bring his brother's killers to book. After years of inquiries and depositions, Joginder had a case in court against the neta who owned the goons that killed Jeet. He wanted Mohammad to testify against him. He had written and phoned several times. Not getting a response, he had asked his father to write.

The lines on Mohammad's face were etched more deeply than ever. His stomach felt tighter than it had all day. He had lost the urge to drink his latte. Leaving it on the table, he made his way out of the cafe. The sun had faded and the sky was the colour of cigarette ash. The shops were deserted. Salespeople were loitering outside, chatting on cellphones. A knot of men was fastened to the glass window of a TV showroom where the game was playing on one of the widescreen TVs. A scrawny dog eyed the men, probably wondering what it was that had the humans so enthralled. The legless beggar and his platform on wheels were nowhere in sight.

Mohammad did not pay attention to any of that as he walked slowly to the parking lot where his car was one of the few left. His mind was full of Jeet and Ram Janak and the neta in the gali. Even now the thought of the neta sent a shiver through him.

A pink flier was stuck to the windscreen of his car; an agitation planned by a local right-wing organisation to protest the killing of cows. He threw it away and drove home on a road that was empty except for stray dogs and cows; the closest Delhi came to a ghost town. Air drifted in through the open car window to tousle his hair. The neem branches drooping above the road twitched restlessly. Somewhere, a television set broke into cheers.

Abhay had invited him over for the match. It was either that, or grappling with his past in his flat. It was a no-brainer.

He tried to recall the names of Abhay's wife and son as he rang the doorbell. Geeta and Nitin? Yes, that was it. Geeta and Nitin.

Geeta answered the doorbell. Unlike her husband, she was small and thin. She was dressed in a pair of old jeans and a creased yellow t-shirt. Her hand rose to smooth her long, dark hair which was mussed up.

'Hi,' she said. The way she spoke made it sound like, But what're you doing here?

'Hi, Abhay said we'd watch the cricket match.'

'Ohhh.' The way she drew out the *oh* meant Abhay hadn't informed her. He probably hadn't expected him to come.

'We haven't put it on yet,' she said. 'Nitin had an accident and we had to take him to the hospital.'

'Oh, no, what happened? I hope he's okay.'

'He's fine. He just fell down and hurt himself. We took him to the emergency room as a precaution, because the bruise was to the head. Do come in.'

She had turned around. It was too late to make an excuse and leave. He shrugged his shoulders and followed her into the drawing room.

It was his first time in their flat. The paintings of forts in Rajasthan on the blue walls and the Rajasthani designs on the silken cushions adorning the sofa and divan reminded him that they were both from Jaipur. Some of the family pictures wore marigold garlands. Those would be the dead relatives. A dark figurine of Nataraja dancing in his circle of fire stood on a low table beside the sofa. A first-aid box sat on the floral carpet, next to the divan, with blood-tinged pieces of cotton wool scattered around it. That was where Nitin must have fallen.

It was obviously a bad time. He wished he hadn't come.

'Please sit down,' Geeta told him.

He settled in the sofa. A packed Wankhade Stadium in Mumbai materialised on the forty-inch plasma TV on the other side of the room. Geeta excused herself, saying Abhay would be along in a minute. She picked up the first-aid box and as much of the cotton wool as she could gather in her hands. The nanny came a little later to clear what was left. Mohammad watched, wishing more than ever that he hadn't come.

Presently Abhay came in and said hi. He had exchanged his white t-shirt for a red one. Possibly the other one had got messed up while taking Nitin to the hospital.

'Hi, I'm sorry about Nitin…,' Mohammad began, springing to his feet.

'Oh, he's okay. Kids do things like that all the time.'

Mohammad was quiet; he wouldn't know since he had no kids. Abhay cocked his head in the direction of the TV. 'How are we doing?' he asked.

'They are thirty for one in the tenth over.'

'Who's out?'

'Tharanga.'

'Who got him?'

'Zaheer.'

'He's the best.'

High praise, especially trotted out for a Muslim? Mohammad had no time to dwell on that as the nanny entered with two glasses of chilled Coke. Abhay and he settled in the sofa and discussed how the game might develop between sips of Coke. The noise surging out of the kitchen suggested lunch was on its way. They wouldn't have eaten, because of Nitin. From the extra place set at the dining table, they expected him to eat with them. He wasn't hungry. But it would be bad form to refuse.

Geeta returned to announce that lunch was ready. She had put on red lipstick and done her hair in a ponytail. He caught a nod as she glanced at Abhay. From the way Abhay relaxed, he concluded she was telling him that Nitin was fine. Kids do things like that all the time, Abhay had said. That translated to they constantly kept their parents on tenterhooks.

The food lay in steel bowls. Mohammad helped Abhay

arrange the chairs so that everyone was facing the TV. There was chicken curry, fried eggplant, dal, roti, rice pulao, and pieces of chopped onion and lettuce. Abhay and Geeta exchanged a look when he helped himself to the chicken curry. He wondered if their Muslim friends suddenly turned vegetarian at their table, thinking the meat might not be halal.

They were having fruit custard for dessert when another Sri Lankan batsman was dismissed. Geeta said she'd better go and relieve the nanny who was watching Nitin. The nanny had the rest of the day off.

After finishing lunch, Mohammad settled in the sofa in front of the TV. Abhay joined him a little later after looking in on Nitin.

'Still only two out?' he said.

'Yeah.'

'Haven't seen the news all day. Mind if we take a look. Maybe someone will be out by the time we come back.'

'Okay.'

Abhay switched the TV over to a news channel. Mohammad started as he recognised the man on the screen. *It was him.* Balding now with sparse silvery hair and a bearlike body stuffed in a cream-coloured Nehru jacket. The shifty eyes were as cold as ever, and the thin lips remained cruel.

They were playing a filetape of him at a school function. An old black and white picture of Jeet from his school graduation flashed on the screen. Then there was Joginder. Unlike Jeet, Joginder was clean-shaven with a haircut. His lined face made him appear much older than his thirty-seven years. He was speaking to the reporter in an office somewhere. A file picture from *The Times of India* of Trilokpuri in the eighties splashed on the screen.

'This guy's a fucking minister in the government,' Abhay's

voice sounded. 'The whole world knows he massacred Sikhs in '84. Yet no one is coming forward to testify against him.'

Abhay was eyeing him, clearly expecting a reaction. His face was packed with outrage. Mohammad ran his tongue nervously over his lips.

'He's a powerful man,' he said.

'So what?'

So what? Surely Abhay wasn't that naïve or reckless? 'You can't be serious, Abhay,' Mohammad said. 'A guy like that can make your life miserable. He's got power, money and God knows how many goondas and policewallahs at his beck and call. Then he has no scruples. He won't stop with you. He'll go after your family without a second thought. Would you want to expose Geeta and Nitin to him?'

Abhay pursed his lips. 'I understand what you're saying,' he said, a little later, 'but if it was me the question would be—do I want my son to live in a world where a monster like that walks scot free? And there I would have to say no.'

The passion in Abhay's voice surprised Mohammad. The guy was dead serious.

He could afford to think like that; he came from the Hindu majority. Even as the thought crossed Mohammad's mind, he realised how nonsensical it was. A crooked politician backed into a corner didn't give a damn whether his detractor was Hindu or Muslim.

Abhay excused himself to answer his cell phone that had started ringing. Before leaving the room, he switched the TV back to the cricket. Mohammad remained where he was.

The exchange with Abhay had brought Jeet into the room. He was sitting in the divan with his bloody face and unruly mane of hair. His eyes, shadowed by blue-black bruises, were watching him; sad, reproachful eyes that were as damning as a pointing finger. Mohammad dropped his gaze.

A whooping Nitin bounded into the room, followed by a harassed-looking Geeta shouting at him to slow down. He appeared none the worse for his injury, except for the unsightly bandage on his head. He headed straight for the divan to extract a tennis ball from under it. '*Nitin*,' Geeta strode forward to snatch the ball from his hands. 'You can only stay if you sit and watch cricket,' she said. 'Otherwise it's back to bed.'

Her finger sliced the air as she finished. Like Ammi's would when laying down the law all those years ago. A sheepish Nitin fetched his small bamboo chair that was placed next to the wall and placed it in front of the TV.

'Good boy,' Geeta said.

She glanced at Mohammad, inclining her head in Nitin's direction. Mohammad nodded to indicate he'd watch Nitin. No sooner had she left the room than Nitin said, with a glance at the doorway, 'Uncle, can I see cartoons?'

Mohammad smiled. If mothers resembled each other then so did kids. How many times had he acted like that once Ammi's back was turned?

'Yes,' he said. 'But keep the volume down. Otherwise Mom will get to know.'

The boy grinned, 'Thanks, Uncle.' Now he was a friend, a co-conspirator against Mom.

Shinchan was playing on the cartoon channel. Nitin devoured it, perched on the edge of his chair like an eagle sitting on a ledge before taking to the air. During a particularly funny exchange, he turned to Mohammad and the two of them laughed out loud.

The little boy's face glowed like a shiny brown orb in the light of the room. There were flashes of white teeth as he rocked with laughter at a gag or a humorous exchange. Despite the ugly bandage on his head, he overflowed with a joy that had not been tempered by tragedy or sullied by bitterness.

An unspeakable sadness surged through Mohammad. He had been like that once, as had Jeet. Jeet's life was snuffed out in Trilokpuri before it could really begin and he had been running from the memory ever since. He had never been able to outdistance it no matter how hard he tried.

Jeet's bruised face was still looming above the divan. His eyes, which were bigger than ever, commanded his attention. They were no longer accusing him. Instead, they were brimming with pain; a pain that went beyond skin, beyond bone. He was staring at a soul that had been torn away from its body to be left twisting and contorting.

Unable to look any longer, he got up and left the room. Abhay was standing outside, talking on his cell phone. 'Mohammad,' he said. Mohammad simply kept going to stop only when he felt Abhay's hand on his shoulder. He turned around.

'I have to go,' he mumbled.

'Is everything alright?' Abhay asked.

Mohammad nodded.

Abhay's face was a mixture of concern and curiosity. He looked as if he was about to say something. But he did not. Instead he stepped back, nodding.

Mohammad walked slowly out of the front door to step out into the street. The street was silent, except for the noise spilling out of TVs that were playing everywhere. He stood there, amidst the parked cars and still trees. He had no idea where to go.

Dried Apricots Smell Like Dead Fish

Pratyaksha

THE BRICK WALL IS DUSTY, faded and broken. It gapes open and you can see the fields for far. Mustard fields. So yellow. Phulo looks out through the gaping wall. The sun is bright. Why then, inside, is everything so dark?

It is already mid-morning. She touches the wall, slides her fingers across, her palm splayed wide.

Daarji* coughs and calls out in a rasping tone, 'Phulo, Phulo.'

Phulo limps as she crosses the courtyard.

The sun is so bright outside. The world seems to be covered with a yellow sheet. And the sky… so blue. As if it is dream time. In the dream, Phulo lies down on the grassy patch near the neem tree. It is a little bit lighter in colour than the surrounding grass. Phulo presses her face in the ground. The grass is rough against her cheek. Rough and green and yet, soft and velvet. A calloused palm cups her face. The rough thumb moves hypnotically in a circular motion on her temples. A tear escapes.

---

*Daarji would literally stand for father. In this story, it is used to refer to Phulo's father-in-law.

It's been so long. But it seems as though it is only yesterday. This is how it was. This is how it is. An ant crawls up her calf, a bee buzzes somewhere, the sun is warm on her body. The grass is sweet. His body was sweet till it was no more. She closes her eyes and breathes his body. Her body is a shell.

Daarji had gone away and thus he was spared. She had pretended to be dead and thus was spared. But this sparing was not life. It was death, worse than death, worse than living. The torture courses through her body every day, every moment.

It has been thirty years. Thirty long years. But if she closes her eyes, it is happening now. The stench of burnt skin fills her. Even now, she cannot look at fire without shivering. So many times while cooking, she has ended up burning her wrists and fingers. Sometimes she has deliberately put her palms above the flame. How does it feel? But within seconds, she draws back her hands. One tiny pinpoint of burn. She can't imagine the fire spreading all over, every inch of the body. He should have died much before. But he didn't. It was one long torturous month. She closes her eyes and his screams fill her whole body. Though towards the end, he had nothing left even to scream. Tears would flow from one eye... the one that was left. One eye that saw the hell this world was. It would have been better if they had shot him or stabbed him. But a quick death was not his destiny. He had to go inch by inch, millimetre by millimetre, body part by body part, the skin, bones, blood.

Phulo believes in destiny. There is no other way to explain the senselessness of what they all went through. All of them. Her own barren life, her own violation. What had we done in our previous lives? Who did we kick, plunder, rape or sodomise?

She sucks on the tiny blob of tobacco. Pushes it beneath her lower lip. Sucks at it like a child sucking at his mother's teats.

She goes back into her room. Baljit looks at her from the picture hung on the wall. His eyes laugh. She remembers his childhood picture that Bebe had once shown her. Baljit, a six-month-old child. So innocent, so beautiful. Did Bebe know that his life would end in such pain? How does anyone know? She thinks so much of death these days. The process of death intrigues her. She is fifty-five now. Daarji is eighty. Bebe would have been seventy-six, Baljit fifty-eight. This house, a hundred. The neighbours, ninety. Their house is empty. Such irony. They still remaining in this house. And them? Gone.

That day the radio had blared so loudly. Baljit had gone to the shop. Bebe had slept in the afternoon. Someone had banged on the door that opened into the courtyard. Satti had come to ask for the hammer. Need to hammer in a nail. Can't find ours.

Then she had conspiratorially lingered on, leaning against the door to say, Indira Gandhi is dead.

They had talked desultorily, expressing anguish.

What the world has come to.

And her own body guard? So it seems.

I have a cousin in the police. He called to tell this.

Baljit came home in the evening. He was tense. He fidgeted with his turban, walked about restlessly in the room, lifting this and keeping that back, sitting and then standing up again.

'Things are not okay. The city was tense,' he said.

'Tense? Why?'

At night, they watched TV while having dinner. There was

bad news everywhere. Delhi was aflame. Baljit checked the door three times. The neighbourhood was quiet.

Bebe admonished him. 'You worry too much, puttar. We have lived here all our lives. We know each one of them. We have been to their homes for births and deaths, weddings and other rituals. We have nothing to fear.'

They were more worried about Daarji. He had gone to Patiala.

Bebe mumbled, 'Call him. From Lalaji's house.'

'They do not have a phone.'

'But the TV and radio are screaming fear.'

Baljit was so restless that he got up thrice.

'Listen, there is some sound, can you hear it?' he asked.

Phulo shut him up. 'It's nothing. Go to sleep. Tomorrow I will go and ask Chaiji if I can make a call from her phone.'

But even she couldn't sleep, kept awake by a swirling emptiness that travelled up from her navel and refused to go away.

The routine has been set over so many years now. Making breakfast, feeding Daarji, going to the shop and spending the whole day there. Earlier, Daarji, too, would sit in the shop. But soon, it became difficult for him. It's been five years now since he stopped going to the shop. He remains at home all alone. Phulo worries over him. If something happens to him in her absence, what will she do? Who will take care? Who will call a doctor? Sometimes, she imagines coming home to find him gone. She is filled with such terror at this thought. She knows it will happen one day. Maybe soon. She will be left alone then.

I am also getting old now, she thinks. Her leg hurts. She limps badly. The bone that got broken then never set properly. Her left eye too. Never got well. She looks at herself in the mirror. Her left eye, dragged down, gives her a crooked look. She touches it slowly.

Why was I spared? I should have died then. My body is all broken and I have been carrying on… Waheguru, spare me now. Spare me the terror.

She has asked her sister if her younger son can come and stay with her. Take over the shop.

It will all be his. The house, the shop. All his. I have no one, Jitti.

Jitti is still thinking about it.

Phulo limps and a sigh works its way up. The shop is a small gift and stationary shop. Back then, it was a big flourishing shop. Big enough to attract attention. Big enough to get burnt down. After the incident, it remained like that for months. Charred and plundered. It was Daarji who had the courage to begin anew. Phulo would have died. Died of pain, died of grief and loneliness, died of hunger, died at all roads ending at a blank wall.

There was nothing for me. There is nothing for me. But sometimes, she is amazed. It is not as if she has not laughed in these thirty years, not lived in these years, not enjoyed good food and good sleep. Not felt rich with emotions.

We are amazing creatures.

She thinks with simple wisdom. Bebe, who would cry so much, would also hold her tight and rock her to sleep in the nights where she screamed out her nightmares.

It was the next day when a crowd gathered. They were not all people from the neighbourhood. They had come from somewhere else. Phulo could see them from the window. Everyone had begun closing their doors. The air was vibrating with hatred. It was an eddy swirling up and entering homes through the cracks in the doors. They were gesturing towards particular houses. They kept gesticulating towards theirs. They had called out Baljit. They had a list. Then Phulo saw Lalaji from next door.

Baljit was reassured.

It's Lalaji, let me go out.

Phulo and Bebe stood by the window. Their hearts in their mouths. Flapping desperately like a caged bird.

They could see Sant Singh, Tayaji (uncle or father's elder brother), from the next lane. There were two more sardarjis. They could not see their faces. Just the colour of their turbans bobbing above the faceless crowd.

And then somebody brought tyres. There was a flash; the crowd had begun to scream. The houses remained shut. Phulo tried to locate Baljit in the sea of faceless people.

And then the crowd moved back. A clearing sprung up in the centre and you could see the dance of fire, the dance of death, gruesome, macabre, brutal. The hellfire let loose.

They wore their garlands bravely. Their hair falling loose was aflame. A golden halo. Their faces were a grotesque scream from hell itself as their skin melted and their torsos burst apart. They ran a naked run engulfed in orange and the crowd finally made way. Till they fell, one by one, in the middle of the road, in front of their homes, in the neighbourhood where they had been born, the lanes that saw them play, the houses where they had gone for food and fun. It was here, amidst their very own, that they died, murdered in the most terrifying death that one can conceive, burnt alive by their very own people who they loved and who had loved them once upon a time.

Phulo fainted. Bebe fainted. The black hole had swallowed them. Life ended that day.

Bebe had died some years after the incident. Her heart had broken. One can die of a broken heart.

To see your child like that, she would often say, 'Just before he fell to the ground, he turned towards our house, looked at the window, knowing that we were standing there. I can still see him looking towards us. He was telling me something. Only, I don't have the heart now to understand his glance. I am the poor damned mother. My womb is barren, like yours is too.'

Bebe would hold Phulo in a tight embrace and the two would rock slowly back and forth, a soft keening cry filling their poor, torn, tortured hearts.

Phulo would often wake up mumbling, Bebe, my skin is burning, Bebe, my chest is hurting. Bebe, cover me up. I am naked, cover me up, Bebe.

In the night, they had barged in. They had pulled her out into the patch beneath the neem tree. They had torn away her salwar, they had clamped her mouth shut with their calloused palms, they had bitten her everywhere, they had burnt her body with their cigarette stubs, they had laughed uproariously when she whimpered with pain. They had taken drunken turns to violate her brutally. They had hit her with sticks, then sodomised her; they had slapped her fiercely and pulled away clumps of hair. She had sunk into the soft earth. Every thrust pushed her deeper into pain unconsciousness. And she screamed Baljit's name every time the pain hit her.

In the morning they found her, naked and bloodied, her leg broken in three places, her eye half torn out, her breasts and stomach burnt. Unconscious and broken like a rag doll but still alive, very much alive.

She had been in hospital for so long. Things had quietened down. There was outrage. The reporters had come. The NGOs had come. The social activists had come. But all too late. Daarji had come immediately to a home that had no soul. Happiness was an elusive bird that had flown away. Forever.

There were other women who were raped. There were other men who had been killed, burnt alive. There were other homes gutted. Lives shattered. They were not alone. But it was the first time for them. And it finished them.

The next-door neighbours had disappeared. The house was locked.

Some woman once came to interview Phulo. She was doing a book on the Sikh riots. Lalaji was one of the accused. Inciting hatred and exhorting the crowd to kill all Sikhs.

Phulo could not believe that. He always used to be so gentle. He would always smile at Baljit; always buy stuff from their shop. He was the elder brother that Daarji trusted with his life. How could he kill Baljit? Baljit had played in his lap.

His Surinder and my Baljit grew up together. Daarji says this even now in amazement.

Satti, Lalaji's bahu and Surinder's wife, was Phulo's friend, almost like her sister. Her son, Anand, spent half the day in their house every day.

The house is now an empty shell. The windows and doors shackled. The garden overrun by weeds. The beams on the shed falling down in ruins. Lalaji had disappeared with his family, absconded.

Phulo has rebuilt her house. Except that wall. She can touch it and feel Baljit. But it has been so long. A lifetime.

There are days when she thinks about nothing. Nothing of that day, nothing of those days. And then days when all thoughts come crawling out of her body, her skin, like maggots. She washes her body constantly; she scrubs her body; she menstruates her body to cleanliness. But the stench of dead fish doesn't leave her body. What will she do of her heart that is trapped in a prison? Her mind moves in a circular fashion along the periphery of her hatred, round and round continuously without break. She looks at others and her blood boils. They killed us. Who are 'they'? She doesn't know. The faceless, nameless people. The crowd. She tries so hard to recall faces. But only one face stands out. Lalaji. And only one smell stands out. That of beedi, tharra and dried apricots. How many there were, she cannot recall. It was so dark. Her body is unclean. Sometimes she wants to leave her body. Get rid of it. It's been so long, yet it is as if only yesterday.

She could kill them all. She doesn't care about Indira Gandhi. She doesn't care about Beant Singh. She doesn't care about anything except her life. Why couldn't it be normal? Ordinary? It is a day like any other. Beginning of winter. The shop is closed today. She is at home. Sitting on the cot in the sun. Doing nothing. Just letting time pass. The tap drips. There is a crow perched on the wall. Daarji sleeps inside. Phulo sits alone. Looking at the shadows creeping into the courtyard. Someone walks over her grave. She shivers. Life will seep away like this.

Someone is knocking at the door. Some young man. She looks at him questioningly, 'Yes?'

'Can I come in?' The young man is hesitant. 'My family knew yours a long time ago.'

She is intrigued. Tries to place him but fails.

'Come in.'

He enters awkwardly. Sits on a stool in the courtyard.

'What is your name? Whose son are you?'

She gets a glass of water.

He looks around.

She goes in to make tea. She looks at him from the kitchen window as the water boils.

He is looking around. Touching a wall, holding a door, walking around, coming back. Not hurried but slowly, pausing, holding, halting. She watches him. Something in his gait holds her attention. Something in the way he holds his head in a particular way.

They sip the tea. He speaks nothing. Just smiles. There is a nervous paleness around his mouth.

He reaches out to touch her hand. 'I am Satish. My mother was your friend.'

'Tell me her name.'

He laughs. 'Didn't you once get lost in the city and couldn't find your way back?'

Phulo starts laughing, 'Oh my goodness, yes. I was so scared.'

He keeps smiling and telling funny things about her past. Her yearnings for khoya and golgappa, her wanting to see the sea, her favourite colour and actor and song and food and what she cooked best.

In the afternoon, as the shadows lengthen, her sweet

innocent past is unfolded in front of her. The courtyard is filled with sunshine and cheer. Phulo laughs and cries and reminisces some more. The gloom evaporates, the walls lose their dank, the corners are filled with laughter.

'Stay tonight,' she tells him.

She cooks a meal for him. The things that she cooks best—rajma, mint chutney, tandoori roti, saag. She cooks with love and attention. As she tempers the vegetables, she smiles. Will he like my food? What his mother said about me, will he believe? But he has yet not told her his mother's name.

That is a surprise, he had whispered.

Daarji asks, 'Is it Jitti's son? Who is it?'

His voice is querulous.

'Daarji, you eat and sleep.'

She feeds the boy lovingly. Take one more roti. She spreads the butter lavishly.

'One more,' she implores.

Even without eating, she is satiated. If I had a son, he would be this old. Her eyes shimmer with unshed tears.

He sleeps like a baby in the night. She tiptoes once to check on him, tucking the razai around his legs. His sleeping face is serene in repose.

And like lightening, it dawns upon her why he looks so familiar. That way of smiling. Her skin crawls. She slumps down.

Satti, he is your son. Satti, you shut the door upon me that day. Satti, your father-in-law, Lalaji, had called Baljit out. You were my sister, you all were family. Who knows that night… your husband too? Who knows? We loved you all and you stabbed us, betrayed us. And now your son is under my roof. How could I feed him? How?

My time to take revenge. Shall I bring the knife from the kitchen? Shall I just drop a burning match on his razai? Let him burn like Baljit. Let him.

Phulo stumbles out. She sits in the courtyard with the cold raining down upon her. She wants to bring a matchstick, a knife… but she is frozen stiff.

Let me die then. Oh, Waheguru let me die now. She collapses on the cold floor. She has been screaming but her voice is gone. She tries to call out to Daarji but no sound comes out.

Someone is picking her up and bringing her inside. Rubbing her soles and palms, covering her with a razai.

'You know who I am? Lalaji died ten years back. Paralysed neck down from a fall.' His voice is sombre. 'They fled away immediately after the riots. Closed up the house and shifted away. There was some inquiry on and off.

'In the beginning, he maintained a strong stand. Defending his actions. Ma would always cry. She would say that we will have to pay for our deeds.

'My elder brother, who was five years old, drowned and died.'

Oh, Anand is dead. My beautiful angel, who would come and demand sweets from me, dead.

'My father lost all his money. The business was all gone. He became an alcoholic.'

He was surely one of them that night. The smell of dry fruits. That's what they dealt in. Yes, he was one of them, apricots.

'Nothing really bad happened to Lalaji. He picked up business once again. This time of sherbets. He lost money. He made money. Everything seemed alright, ordinary, till he fell from the terrace of the half-built new house. Towards the end, he would scream in terror, "The fire, does it burn your body into ash?"

'He became obsessed with fire. He would cower in his bed and cry like a child. Don't burn my body. His voice would wail in a whimpering cry.'

He should have been burnt alive, yes, burnt alive to feel the pain that he inflicted on others.

'I was born much later. But, tell me, why did my mother suffer so much? She loved you always and she lives a life of guilt and suffering. Chaiji, she has suffered no less than you. Our family was finished after that incident. She always talks about you, about the life that she had and you had before the happening. The wonderful bond that you all shared.

'Why did it have to end like this? She cannot fathom. I have seen this house through her, every nook and corner, I know of the things that you have done together during the winter afternoons, making pickle and potato chips, knitting sweaters and caps.

'She loves you and she feels if you forgive us, our life will mend. Lalaji is gone. Anand is gone. My dadi is gone. Only we are left and you are left Chaiji, the survivors.

'I have come to seek forgiveness. My mother asked me to say this, forgive her, forgive them. In God's name, forgive them.'

Phulo has turned to stone. She covers her ears with her palms. She sways lightly. Her face is puckered. She whimpers, I am dead, I am dead, I am dead. The earth is red with my blood. The grass is all burnt and the blood has rusted. Satti, I am dead. Satti, we are all dead.

Among One's Own

Harish Narang

Translated from the original Hindi by the author

IT WAS A HOT MAY afternoon. As he exited the Vikas Sadan building, his head reeled under the punishing sun. He felt like boarding a bus and heading straight home. But he had to go get his reading glasses made. He had been having a lot of trouble reading ever since he had misplaced them during a seminar in Shimla. Whenever he read something in class or at home, he had to take off his distance glasses and bring the reading material close to his eyes in order to decipher the words. It put a lot of strain on his eyes and soon they'd begin watering. He was forced to wash his eyes when that happened, arousing recrimination from his wife and daughter.

'Is this the right way to go about your reading? Go and get new glasses made,' his wife had admonished him that very morning.

'Papa, you once said that the optician is a friend of yours. So why don't you go enjoy his hospitality and order your new glasses?' his daughter had added.

He had come to the DDA office in the Vikas Sadan building to deposit the ground rent for his apartment. After doing that, he was determined to order his new reading glasses. His friend Harjeet's shop, Bami Opticals, was nearby.

Harjeet was quite a character. He was hardly the typical shopkeeper type. Whenever Mahesh visited his shop, he rarely ever found him there. During the summer, he could be found at the Shyam Juice Corner downing a glass of fresh sugarcane juice along with the local gossip. During the winter, he was parked at the Verghese Coffee House, savouring filtered coffee with a plate of steaming idlis. Whenever a customer arrived at his shop, his assistant would set off to inform him. Earlier, Harjeet's daarji or father managed the shop but for the last few years he had stopped coming, possibly due to his advancing age and ill health, which left Harjeet free to handle the business independently. Since then, Harjeet had become the general secretary of the market shopkeepers' association. Upon entering his shop, the first thing you saw on the wall in front of you was a framed group photo of the association members with Prime Minister Indira Gandhi. To the left of Mrs Gandhi sat Durjan Dass, the president of the association, and to her right was seated Harjeet. The two of them also worked in the youth wing of Mrs Gandhi's Congress party.

Mahesh's association with Harjeet went back over twenty-five years; that was why he was more of a friend than a customer. Sometimes the two would converse over glasses of sugarcane juice; sometimes over platefuls of golgappe or chaat. A good conversation was the bonus for getting your spectacles made from him. Harjeet was a big gossipmonger. Once he started, he would not let Mahesh leave until the next customer arrived. In those days Mahesh, too, had ample time on his hands. He was not into seminar-mania yet and some distance away from drowning himself in a pond of book writing. He would listen patiently as Harjeet finished narrating one story and then moved on to another immediately thereafter.

'Professor Sahib, this home minister of ours is a khaati by caste. Professor Sahib, you understand khaati, no?' Without waiting for an answer, Harjeet was off and running, 'A khaati is a tarkhaan.' While Mahesh was still figuring out the meaning of tarkhaan, Harjeet plunged ahead, 'My daarji had seen it with his own eyes. He used to make charpoys. Yes, Professor Sahib, charpoys, that is, beds... once he became a minister, he left his bebe – wife – behind in the village. And then sometimes he would take up with a begum from Malerkotla or a mutiar – damsel – from Dera Bassi.'

Harjeet had no qualms about the fact that he was making fun of a very senior leader of his party who was also a distinguished member of his own community. Nor was he conscious of the fact that Mahesh had no knowledge about the mutiars of Dera Bassi. In between, he'd sometimes ask, for the sake of asking, as to what was happening at Mahesh's university, 'Professor Sahib, when will the next strike take place? For long, we haven't heard any scandal about your university. What happened to that student who used to pry into the girls' hostel rooms with his army binoculars?'

Before Mahesh could reply, Harjeet would have started on another story. Mahesh revisited all this in his head as he crossed the path that led from the Vikas Sadan building to the underground passage in the relentless heat. Descending the stairs that led to the underground passage, he suddenly recalled Harjeet's friend, Durjan Dass. Along with Harjeet and other shopkeepers, Durjan Dass had struggled for years to have the underground passage constructed. After the construction of a flyover over the nearby railway line, the traffic had begun moving at great speed because of which the people living in the INA Colony flats across the road began shying away from approaching the market. An accident in which a small child was killed by a speeding vehicle while crossing the road merely accentuated that trend. The market's business took a major hit. Taking advantage of the situation, a Bihari man set up a temporary shed against the wall of a flat to sell bread, eggs, butter, and other essential goods. Then a tea stall opened in a temporary brick structure while a Munna Hair Dressing Saloon started operating under a banyan tree. Mahesh recalled vividly the days when Harjeet would talk to him in detail about the need for an underground passage. Although Mahesh did not know anyone in the traffic police or the New Delhi Municipal Counsil (NDMC), he told Harjeet, 'Remember, any request for the installation of traffic lights, construction of an overbridge or an underground passage is considered seriously only after a certain number of accidents have taken place there.'

That hadn't discouraged either Harjeet or his friend Durjan. And now that the underground passage was ready, Durjan was not around to savour the success of their struggle or make political capital out of it. He had been caught up in the violence and mass murder of Sikhs that ensued following the murder of Mrs Gandhi. The friendship between Harjeet and Durjan had also suffered, as a result.

It was while sitting in his shop that manufactured iron grills, doors, and windows that Durjan was assassinated. Even several years later, his killers had not been identified and arrested much in the same way the murderers of thousands of Sikh men, women and children had not been caught, although the qatle-aam had taken place for three days and nights in the presence of hundreds of people, just like the one engineered hundreds of years ago by the zaalim, Nadir Shah. The only difference was that this had occurred under the very nose of the police deployed to save the lives of innocent people and, finally, the Army had flag-marched through the entire city to put an end to the killing and looting. In the aftermath, some held the political leaders responsible while others the police force. But Mahesh believed that the citizens of Delhi were the ones to blame. When the murders were taking place, the entire city had closed its eyes to them. When people were being burnt alive or killed by crushing them under the wheels of vehicles, even the media reports were muted. Of course, there had been a few isolated attempts to save people here and there and that had been publicised by the government. Mahesh recalled fully well that there had been no incidents of violence in his university, but that was an exception to the rule. Although the goons from the neighbourhood had repeatedly tried to enter the campus, the vigilance teams, comprising students, teachers, and administrative staff, had foiled all their attempts, thus saving not only the Sikhs on campus but also the students and staff of a neighbouring school that was run by a Sikh organisation. Harjeet's son Jugnu – his real name was Gagandeep but everyone called him Jugnu out of love – also studied in the school and Mahesh recalled vividly how disturbed Harjeet had been when the school decided to send the children home under police escort.

What happened to us then, Mahesh wondered, recalling the words that Pandit Jawaharlal Nehru uttered during the riots that accompanied Partition: 'Our people have gone mad'. Yes, they had indeed gone mad. Some displayed their beastliness, while others closed their eyes to it.

Coming out of the underground passage, Mahesh felt his throat parching and hurried to get a cold drink upon reaching the shop. There would be snacks of political gossip to partake as well.

'Professor Sahib, all this is false propaganda. Scindia never called the BJP anti-national... This Ajit Singh will vanquish VP Singh. Take it from me, in the next cabinet reshuffle, Buta Singh will be appointed the Home Minister... for sure.' Whether Durjan Dass's wife got a ticket in the next Metropolitan Council election, or whether the Kashmiri militants would free Doraiswamy were some of the issues on which Harjeet would air his opinion.

Upon entering the market, Mahesh looked up, as always, at the signboard of Bami Opticians. There was a picture of a beautiful, fair girl wearing a big, rectangular frame over eyes that seemed to look you straight in the eye. Below it, a short phrase was written in English, *Bami Opticians: For A New Vision In Your Life*. This phrase always caught Mahesh's fancy; he did not know why. Anyway, now the picture and the writing below had got blurred with the passage of time. It had been there for more than twenty-five years. During this time, even the real visions of people's lives had got blurred, Mahesh thought, and this was only a lifeless signboard made of wood and paint. His eyes travelled down from the signboard to make out the closed door and the thick, brass padlock hanging on it. The lock was similar to the one he had at home. Moving forward for a closer look, he got the impression that the shop had been closed for many days. Pieces of paper, empty packets of cigarettes, paan masala, and dry leaves lay strewn in the corners of the corridor.

Apparently, the place had not been swept for many days. God forbid, if Harjeet's daarji... He tried his best not to complete the thought. Instead, he attempted to focus his thoughts on what he had come to do from the Vikas Sadan building to this place.

'Come, Professor Sahib, come here. It is so hot, no!'

The owner of the next shop – Duggal Provision Store – Lala Thakur Dass had noticed him standing there. Because of Harjeet, Mahesh had also come to know some of the shopkeepers in the neighbourhood. Half reclining with the help of a pillow on a steel-framed, wovenstring bed in the corridor, Lalaji motioned for him to sit on the steel chair kept nearby and called out to his servant, 'Oye, Bishan-a, bring a glass of cold water for Professor Sahib.' Then he turned to Mahesh and said, 'It's so hot, sir. And there is no sign of any rains as yet. Shri Ram Ji, be merciful, don't know what will happen to the nation. They say it is far worse in Bihar and UP. But in Assam and Bengal, the rivers are flooding. Is it true, Professor Sahib? I tell you, the real reason is the increasing population... these Christians and Muslims, Professor Sahib, mark my words, if we don't do anything drastic, let alone heat and floods, there will be one day when another division of the nation will happen.'

Like Harjeet, Lala Thakur Dass would not stop once he started talking. Mahesh was dying to know as to why and for how long had Harjeet's shop been closed. Lalaji, however, was busy riding his favourite hobby horse. Mahesh was sure that if he did not do anything soon, Lalaji would go on to narrate the full history of India's partition as he had done many times before. Lalaji had an old newspaper in one hand that he was using as a fan to cool himself. Mahesh suspected that Lalaji had not mentioned anything about Harjeet's closed shop deliberately. But why? In between, Bishan had come and handed him a steel glass full of cold water from which emanated the sweet scent of an earthen pot. The heat was now really oppressive. So Mahesh decided to drink the water first. After emptying the glass and keeping it on the floor near the foot of his chair, he asked Lalaji, 'Lalaji, this shop of Harjeet's...'

Lalaji did not let him complete the sentence. 'Ji, they have left. Sold the shop. It has been, Shri Ramji look after our well-being, more than a month and a half. A shopkeeper from this very market has bought the shop – Garib Dass. The one who owns shop number eighteen. Says he'll open a video games parlour. Professor Sahib, these days only such new businesses are thriving. Put up a couple of machines and charge two-three rupees from children for a couple of minutes. By the evening you have two hundred and fifty rupees or more in your kitty. Nothing sold, nothing bought, but the returns are fantastic. Garib Dass's son will man the shop. Yes, the same who was caught copying in his class seven examination.'

Mahesh wasn't listening to him. He wondered as to how Harjeet had taken such a sudden decision. He had never mentioned it before. The shop earned good money. Of late, he had also started manufacturing the lenses himself. He said he had hired a place in Arjun Nagar near his residence for the purpose. His daarji praised Delhi and Delhiites to no end, 'Professor Sahib, Wahe Guru bless them, these people not only provided us with clothing, food, shelter, housing, but also owned us. Now even marital ties are being established between them and us.'

'But, Lalaji, why suddenly this?' he began. Lala Thakur Dass again cut him short.

'Professor Sahib, the fact is that after the '84 killings, he felt unsettled. He didn't say anything but from his behaviour and other things, it was amply clear. You know, of course, that there was horrendous rioting around his residence in Arjun Nagar, where Durjan Dass also lived. Somehow, Harjeet's house escaped the wrath of the goons, but he still felt betrayed. It was this that led to differences between him and Durjan Dass. Otherwise, you know very well how close they were. Together, they did so much for the market. And now both of them are gone.'

Interrupting this unending discourse, Mahesh said, 'But Lalaji, before leaving he must have given a reason for this, must have mentioned as to where he was going, what he would do.'

'Ji, he's gone to Ambarsar along with his entire family. Said that he'd go live among his own. They say he put up a factory for manufacturing lenses. He had the machines and wherewithal with him. He had gone and seen the place earlier. Perhaps also paid some "advance".'

'But, Lalaji, there must have been a specific reason for taking such a decision suddenly?'

Lalaji turned towards Durjan Dass's shop, then looked in the direction of the Verghese Coffee House before saying in a low voice, 'How to put it, Professor Sahib? There are as many speculations as are people around. Ever since the killing of Durjan Dass, people have been saying all kinds of things. They did not say it to his face but many also named Harjeet. Anyway, let's leave it. He wanted to go settle among his own, so he decided. Also, some aged relative of his was caught recently in the VIP area with a can of kerosene oil and some documents, etc., too, were recovered. They say it was reported on the radio and TV. I did not see it but it was talked about in the market. After that, Harjeet made up his mind. One day, I came here in the morning to find that his shop had been bought by Garib Dass. Harjeet and he were quite close. Professor Sahib, you know that Harjeet would often be at the chaat kiosk in front of his shop... They say it was sold for twenty-seven though the papers had been signed for only three-and-a-half. Anyway, let's leave it. How does it matter? My son Prem said, "If Uncle had talked to us, we'd also have been ready to buy." For some time, he has been wanting to open a beauty parlour. Anyway, it's all a matter of luck. Let Harjeet be happy among his own.'

Lalaji was once again riding his hobby horse, but Mahesh's mind was on Harjeet's decision to go settle in Punjab. After Partition, Harjeet's daarji had come down from Rawalpindi and settled in Delhi. As he used to say, he had adopted Delhi and Delhiites had adopted him… and now, Harjeet had gone to Amritsar to go and settle among his own people!

'Okay, Lalaji, I'll leave now. If Harjeet comes visiting, tell him to meet me as well.'

Mahesh picked up his briefcase and started to leave.

'Yes, sure, I'll tell him. Why don't you stay for a cup of tea, Professor Sahib?'

Mahesh thanked him and said he will do so some other time, before leaving in the direction of the bus stop. While waiting for the bus, he wondered if it was not a part of some bigger game. Wasn't there a force that wanted not only India but every major nation to splinter into dozens of pieces? Everywhere, people believing in different religions, speaking different languages, setting up their own small regimes, their own small nests, and then fighting and cutting each other's throats to save their fiefs from attacks by outsiders...

Serbia-Bosnia, Azerbaijan-Armenia, Russia-Chechnya, Sindhi-Mohajir, Pashtun-Tajik, Hindu-Sikh, Sunni-Shia, Catholic-Protestant, Tamil-Sinhala, Sawaran-Dalit, Mandir-Masjid, to each his dulcimer and to each his song! But wasn't there a single sootradhar, a narrator, for all of them?

'Okay, Mahesh, now look for a new optician. You know, the one with another new vision!' Mahesh told himself and took out a five-rupee note to buy a copy of the *Evening Times.* Just then, the Route 511 bus came and he boarded it. The bus was practically empty; so he was able to get a seat immediately. After sitting down, he took off his distance glasses, put them in his pocket and began reading the headlines of the newspaper: *Rioting at Scindia House.* Towards the left, the small lead read: *Terrorists loot bank in Punjab, seven killed.* Towards the right was: *Amina deposes before the court.*

Mahesh had a lot of difficulty reading without his reading glasses, which was why he had come to get a new pair. He decided to read the details of the news at leisure, while lying in his bed, after reaching home. He folded the newspaper and kept it to one side, and took out his distance glasses to put them on again. The bus had reached the All India Institute of Medical Sciences. Mahesh recalled the mob that had collected there after the killing of Mrs Gandhi. It was from there that the killings that were going on, even after several years, emanated. Every day, scores of innocent people got killed. Now the poison had spread even to the Terai region of Uttar Pradesh. In fact, the people had got so used to news of killings that they hardly paid any attention to them. Suddenly, he recalled the news item about the looting of the bank and the killings published in the *Evening Times.* Once again, he took off his glasses and put them in his pocket, and opened the newspaper to begin reading:

This morning, terrorists attacked a senior branch of the Punjab and Sind Bank in Amritsar, and looted fifteen lakh rupees and killed seven people, including the guard. The terrorists fled in a white Maruti car. While fleeing, they took the rifle of the guard along with them. Among those dead was a businessman from Delhi, who had come to withdraw some money. The condition of two of the injured is...

The newspaper slipped from Mahesh's hand and fell near the seat. The passenger in the next seat was surprised that he made no effort to pick it up.

Karma

Aditya Sharma

IN THE EARLY EIGHTIES, WE were living in a rented house in Rohtash Nagar in East Delhi. My father had migrated to Delhi from his village in Punjab's Ropar district some fifteen years ago. He worked as a taxi driver. Working long hours every day, he managed to buy his own taxi within three years of his arrival in Delhi. A few years later, he sold his taxi and bought a matador to take students to and from school. Soon enough, he purchased one more matador and hired two drivers. His business flourished and he also bought a second-hand Ambassador car. Over the past year, he had been busy constructing our house in adjoining Babarpur, which was about one-and-a-half kilometres from Rohtash Nagar. We learnt that we would be moving into our new house soon.

Tall and wellbuilt, my father cut a striking figure with his jet-black beard and turbaned head. He had a high-pitched voice. When he spoke, we could hear him in the next room and even outside the house. I was the eldest of the three children and my father doted on me a lot. He fondly called me Raj, short for Rajinder Kaur, my official name.

Being good at studies, I helped my six-year-old sister Parvinder and four-year-old brother Inderjeet with their school work. They addressed me as 'Teacher Didi'. On 1 October 1984, while we were returning home from school, they pointed out a truck parked outside our house. I realised that my father and his drivers were putting our household items into the truck to shift to our new house.

There were several hundred Sikh families living in Rohtash Nagar. Most of them had settled there following Partition. We had celebrated our festivals with our Sikh neighbours and prayed at gurudwaras together. Now that we were leaving them, we felt quite lost. At the same time, we also felt excited. We were finally going to have a home of our own.

We had discarded our old furniture and bought a new set of beds, a dining table and chairs to decorate our new home. In Babarpur, our immediate neighbours were Hindus but there were about half-a-dozen Sikh families too, including our two distant relatives—the Bainses and the Randhawas. Mr Balbir Randhawa, who was in his early thirties, was my mother's cousin. He lived with his family at the far-end of the lane where our house was located. Mr Bhagat Ram Bains was in his early fifties and he lived with his wife and son across the broad road passing behind our house. The road was so broad that it had aptly been named 'Sau Foota', meaning hundred-feet wide. The Bainses were referred to as 'Cut Sard' and 'Mona Sikhs', which meant their men folk had trimmed their hair and didn't keep beards.

I often noticed that my father left water and grains of wheat and rice for sparrows before going to work. 'Why do you feed them?' I asked him one day.

'Puttar, they are hungry,' my father smiled at me. 'They ask me to give them something to eat.'

'You can talk to them?' I asked him in disbelief.

'Yes, Raj,' my father guffawed, running his hand through his beard.

It was amazing! The sparrows could talk to my father! A few days later, when I tried talking to them, they flew away in fright.

On Sundays, my father would take the entire family to Gurudwara Bangla Sahib in the car and tell us about the inspiring lives of the Sikh gurus on the way. During our holidays, he would drive us all the way to his village in Punjab. In the company of my grandparents, uncles and cousins, we used to have such a wonderful time that I would often pray these happy days should never go away.

On 31 October 1984, while returning from school, I heard that Prime Minister Indira Gandhi had been assassinated by her own security guards. They were two Sikhs. Even though I was just a ten-year-old, I could sense that the carefree expression people wore the day before had been replaced with a sense of numbness. It looked as if they had lost one of their relatives. The shock was also apparent in the sombre tone of the TV and radio commentators who were giving the news of the assassination to the country. The next morning, the front page of all the newspapers were filled with Indira Gandhi. Putting the Hindi daily on the table, my father sighed, 'This shouldn't have happened.'

At about 9 a.m., he left home to meet one of his drivers. I waved him goodbye. He sat down in the car but then shook his head as if recollecting something. He got out of the car, locked its door and said to me, 'Tell your mother that I am going to visit Mamaji's house to enquire about his elder brother.' He was referring to Mr Bains, whose brother had been diagnosed with cancer. He had come from Punjab and was being treated at the AIIMS hospital. Like our parents, we kids also called Mr and Mrs Bains Mamaji and Mamiji, even though they were old enough to be our grandparents.

Because of Indira Gandhi's assassination, schools had been closed. I was playing hopscotch (we called it stapu) with my siblings outside our house when we heard indistinct voices from a distance. It looked as if some people were protesting. Curious, I ran up to the roof of our house and saw smoke rising from a nearby school, about five hundred metres away.

Just then, Mr Jagdish Aggarwal, our next-door neighbour, rushed into our house. Sensing something wasn't right, I followed him inside. Mr Aggarwal was telling Mother that there had been incidents of violence against Sikhs in our locality. Pointing at the smoke, he said, 'A mob is burning the school there.' The school belonged to a prominent Sikh businessman, who made the then popular Texla TV. 'A few Sikh houses in neighbouring localities have been attacked.' Mr Aggarwal added, 'Don't allow Mr Singh to go out today.'

Hearing this, my mother stopped kneading the flour. Wiping her hands with her dupatta, she said to me, 'I am going to Mamaji's place to warn your father to remain there. Take care of your siblings. I'll be back soon.' Very few people in the locality had landline telephone connections those days. Although Mr Bains had a telephone, we didn't have one. My mother could only rush to Mr Bains's house to apprise my father about the violence.

As Mother left, we could hear a mob chanting slogans. They were praising Indira Gandhi. Once again, I climbed onto the roof of our single-storey house. The smoke from the burning school had now become thicker. As I looked around, I could see smoke billowing from four or five different places in our locality.

A few minutes later, I saw Mother rushing back into the house. She bolted all the doors in a state of urgency. Her face had turned very pale. I could see her lips quivering. I had never seen her so panic-stricken. It was obvious that she had seen something terrible. She knelt down on the floor, and started praying to god feverishly. Before she could even compose herself, we heard Mr Aggarwal knocking at the window that faced the street. 'Behenji,' he called out, 'the mob is advancing. Come into my house immediately.'

There was a note of anxiety in his voice. Stunned, my mother opened the door and we followed Mr Aggarwal into his house right across the street. We sat in the drawing room, which had a window through which we could look at our house. Mrs Aggarwal (we called her Poonam Aunty) got a cup of tea for Mother and some biscuits for us. 'There are about three to four groups of men on rampage in the locality,' explained Mr Aggarwal. 'I can recognise only two or three people in them, most of them are outsiders.'

Suddenly, my mother got up from the chair, leaving the tea in her cup unfinished. 'Hai Rabba,' she cried, 'How could I forget Veerji?' She was referring to our uncle Mr Balbir Randhawa, who lived a few houses away. 'What if the mob enters his house from the back side?' my mother said, horrified, 'I need to go and warn him.' Turning to Aunty, she said to her, 'Poonam, please take care of my children. I'll be back soon.'

'Behenji, why are you risking your life?' asked Mr Aggarwal. 'What if someone in the mob recognises you?'

'If I don't warn my brother, who will?' asked my mother and walked into the adjoining room with Poonam Aunty. When she came out, she was dressed in Aunty's clothes and was wearing a few bangles on both her wrists. 'I don't think I can be identified now,' my mother said to Mr Aggarwal.

My mother then unfastened the cloth used for tying my brother's hair in a bun. She combed his hair and tied it in two small braids. 'Inder, you look like your sisters now,' my mother told him firmly. Turning to Poonam Aunty, she added, 'Nobody can make out now that he is a Sikh boy.' Inderjeet resented being turned into a girl, but Mother promised him that if he co-operated, she would ask Papa to get him a box of Five Star chocolates.

When Mother left, I stood on the divan and looked at our house through the window covered by a jaali. One could see through the window without being seen from outside, unless of course, someone switched on the light in the room. Or if someone from outside came very close to the jaali and peeped inside. I saw a group of about twenty men, carrying iron rods and lathis, gathered on the street. A man pointed at our house. The others around him nodded.

Soon, the rioters marched into our house. I saw many of them coming out and walking off with our TV, refrigerator, furniture, gas cylinder, stove, utensils, chairs, tables—practically everything they could lay their hands on. One of the men even took away my doll. Another had a few statues of flamingos in his hands that my mother had bought to decorate our home for Diwali. I wanted to scream at those men to keep our things back, but knew it would be suicidal.

After emptying our house, the mob set it on fire. Then someone pointed at our car. On the back window of the car, my father had pasted the sticker of the Khanda—the sacred sign of the Sikhs. It has a double-edged sword with a circle on it and two single-edged swords. The mob instantly recognised that the car belonged to a Sikh. Raining blows with iron rods on the car, the mob first broke its windshield, back and side windows. I then saw a man opening the bonnet and extracting the petrol in a canister. He doused the car with the petrol and set it on fire. Unable to see flames leaping out of both our house and car, I collapsed on the divan. I was so numb that even tears refused to come from my eyes. As I lay, my brother came near me and my sister began rubbing my forehead with her tiny fingers. Even at their young age, they had the ability to understand that their sister was in a state of shock. It felt better just to lie on the bed with my siblings beside me. We could hear men screaming, 'Khoon ka badla khoon', 'Indira Gandhi amar rahein.'

I lay in bed for a long time. Poonam Aunty nudged me to get up. She was carrying food for us. Soon, the sloganeering subsided but I could see Mr Aggarwal keeping a strict watch on the main gate. It was about 4 p.m., and, except for some biscuits, we hadn't eaten anything since morning. As Poonam Aunty offered some rice and sabzi to me, I realised that I was too dazed to eat anything. Aunty insisted. I forced some rice down my gullet and helped my siblings to eat.

Suddenly, I heard the drumming of several feet on the ground. Before we knew it, a mob comprising about a dozen men had forcibly entered Mr Aggarwal's house. They were brandishing swords, knives and iron rods.

A hefty, dark-skinned man in his early thirties, who looked like the leader of the mob, stood in front of Mr Aggarwal and hollered, 'I know you have hidden your Sikh neighbours here.

Tell them to come out, otherwise it won't be good for you.'

'Who told you that?' asked Mr Aggarwal. Even if he was nervous, he didn't show it. 'I haven't sheltered any Sikhs here.'

'If I find even a single Sikh,' the man threatened Mr Aggarwal, 'don't blame me if my men crack open your head.'

The dark man signalled to his accomplices. Clutching their weapons, the men began looking under the beds, in the bathroom, toilet and storeroom. These men were speaking in a rustic way. From their appearance, it was obvious that they did odd jobs to make ends meet and belonged to poor families. Some of them looked drunk. I saw three men going to the terrace while two men entered the drawing room where I was helping my siblings to eat. I felt so stunned by the sight of these dishevelled men with bloodshot eyes that I could suddenly feel my heart beating furiously. Putting their swords on the table, they searched behind the doors and the divan. They even made Mr Aggarwal open the almirah.

The men who had gone to check on the roof came down looking frustrated. 'Nobody up there,' said one of them.

'Your daughters?' a man in the mob pointed at us.

'Yes,' said Mr Aggarwal.

Satisfied, the leader motioned to his men and all of them went away as abruptly as they had come. Poonam Aunty came into our room and hugged us lovingly but I was so traumatised that the comfort she was trying to provide failed to have any effect on me.

A few minutes later, when my mother returned, I sat beside her holding her hand tightly. When she learnt about the mob, her body shook with anger. 'Nobody can kill those who are protected by God,' she exclaimed, even as tears rolled down her cheeks.

After a short pause, she said to Aunty, 'I managed to inform Veerji just in time. He and his family escaped to Sharmaji's house minutes before a mob surrounded his house.'

Thirty-two years have passed since then, but even now I can't forget the men who barged into Mr Aggarwal's house. I often find myself recalling the images of their naked swords lying on the table and the depraved look in their eyes. Had my mother not tied my brother's hair in two braids and made him look like a girl, I shudder to think what would have happened.

As night fell, my mother said to Aunty, 'We are going to Mr Bains's house to be with Sardarji.' Mummy was referring to my father. She thanked the Aggarwals for putting their lives at risk to save us. Taking Inderjeet in her arms, she motioned for me and Parvinder to follow her.

'Wait,' said Mr Aggarwal, 'The rioters are out there. I will escort you to the house. If anyone questions us, I will say we are going to visit Mr Vivek Bansal. You know Vivek, my brother-in-law, who also lives across the Sau Foota road?'

We managed to reach our uncle's place without being accosted. My eyes eagerly searched for my father. The Bains, as I have mentioned before, were Mona Sikhs, and the male members didn't sport beards or long hair. Mamaji and Mamiji, together with their son, were seated on the chairs at the dining table. I noticed two clean-shaven men seated on the sofa. Maybe, my father would be joining us soon, I thought.

I was startled out of my wits when I heard my father call my name. With a shock that I remember to this day, I realised that one of the 'clean-shaven men' on the sofa was my father! His turban and beard were gone and he looked such a different man. 'It's all god's will,' I heard him console my mother.

I went up to my father and hugged him tightly, missing for the first time the rugged feel of his beard on my face. Tears began falling from my eyes. 'Raj, be brave,' my father admonished me, 'Don't cry.' In a conspiratorial tone, he whispered in my ear, 'If you cry, who will take care of your brother and sister?'

I forced myself to calm down. As my hand touched his shoulders and arms, I was comforted by the feel of their familiar muscular build. Even then it took me some time to believe that he was indeed my father. And then as the other clean-shaven man spoke, I realised that he was our uncle, Mr Balbir Randhawa.

'We had to trim our hair and shave off our beards,' he explained to my mother, 'The mobs were searching each house and there was no telling when they would force their way into Mr Sharma's house, where you left me. Mr Sharma managed to get a barber for me. After he had cut my hair and shaved off my beard, I got him to Mr Bains's house.' Pointing at my father, Balbir Uncle added, 'He trimmed Mr Ram Singh's hair and shaved off his beard too. Do you know how much he charged? Rs 500 per person!

'As soon as the barber left, a mob of ten armed men entered Mr Bains's house. They searched all the rooms, bathroom and toilet. Ram Singh and I jumped into the adjacent house, which is locked from outside, and hid there. Somebody must have informed the mob that Mr Bains might have sheltered Sikhs. Fortunately, they didn't look into this.' Balbir Uncle picked up a sack lying in a corner of the room and opened it for all of us to see. 'Look, the barber had put Ram Singh's hair in it!'

'Where are your wife and sons?' my mother asked Balbir Uncle.

'They are still at Mr Sharma's house,' my father replied for Balbir Uncle.

As night fell, my siblings fell asleep on the sofa, but the elders continued to stay awake and spoke in whispers. Outside, the rioters were shouting the names of the Sikhs hiding in the neighbourhood, demanding they come out. I heard the rioters calling my father's and Balbir Uncle's names several times. Scared as never before, we spent the rest of the night imagining the worst. 'If something happens to me,' Balbir Uncle said to my mother, 'Tell my wife to go back to Punjab and settle there with the kids.'

Even as we were hoping that the violence would end the next day, the killing and looting continued unabated. It was 2 November, the second day of the riots. Mr Ravi Chauhan, the Bains's next-door neighbour, knew we were hiding in the house. He worked as a customs officer and was a good friend of Mr Bains. He informed us that the mob was searching for Sikhs with the help of the voter list. 'Where are the police?' fumed Balbir Uncle. 'The government knows about the riots, but instead of stopping the mobs, it's instigating them.'

'Going by the frenetic search for Sikhs in the locality,' said Mr Chauhan, 'it's likely that the mob will get you sooner or later. I have learnt that the rioters are quite suspicious of Mr Bains.'

'What do we do then?' asked Balbir Uncle, biting his lips.

'Before the mob finds us,' my father said, 'we must escape.'

'Is it even possible?' asked Balbir Uncle.

'I have an idea,' said Mr Chauhan, 'My mother has just undergone heart surgery at Safdarjung Hospital. You two,' he pointed at my father and Balbir Uncle, 'come with me in my car. If the rioters ask us where we are going, I'll tell them that you are my cousins and we are visiting my mother. I'll also take my wife along. It will help us look like a family.'

'But we have turban marks on our foreheads,' said Balbir Uncle, 'we might get recognised.'

'If we want to get out of here,' said my father, 'we need to take the risk.'

'Aren't we safe here?' asked Balbir Uncle.

'Safe here?' my father exclaimed. 'You know Mr Bains is under suspicion. And what if the barber who has cut our hair gives us away? The mob already knows that we are alive and hiding in one of the houses. It's just a matter of time before they ferret us out.'

Sensing good reasoning in my father's words, Balbir Uncle agreed, 'You do have a point, but…'

'Shorn of our hair and beards,' interrupted my father, 'we stand a good chance to escape.'

'Your wife and kids are somewhat safe here,' Mr Chauhan said to my father and Balbir Uncle. 'They can mingle easily with the Bains and Sharma families. The mob is particularly looking for men.'

'Could you drive us to Vivek Vihar?' my father asked Mr Chauhan. 'To Lala Kuddamal's house?'

Lalaji, as we all called him, was a close friend of Father's. He was a businessman who printed elaborate designs in gold and silver on saris. My father had often transported his saris to Lalaji's customers in his matadors. Both his house and factory were located in Vivek Vihar's Jhilmil Industrial Area, which was about seven kilometres from Babarpur.

'Yes, I can,' said Mr Chauhan. 'Provided we are able to get out of the locality. The mob has sealed off the exit roads with big stones.'

'Don't worry about the stones,' said Mr Bains. 'I'll ask my friends in the neighbourhood to remove them when you leave.'

'I could have suggested that you escape tonight,' explained Mr Chauhan, 'but if we get caught at night, the mob won't even listen to us.'

Next morning, at about ten, my father and Balbir Uncle got a signal from Mr Chauhan to come out of the house. Tears welled up in my mother's eyes as Father extricated his hand from hers and told her to take care of us children. She knew that it could be the last time that we were all together.

My mother and I stood beside the window covered by a jaali and looked at my father and Balbir Uncle walking towards Mr Chauhan's white Fiat car. They sat down in the backseat; Mr and Mrs Chauhan were seated in the front. Mr Chauhan turned the key in the ignition. The engine cranked a couple of times but didn't start. The horrified passengers of the car looked at each other as they could see a group of twenty men about hundred metres away.

'Damn it,' Mr Chauhan exclaimed in frustration, 'the car seemed fine when I reversed it.'

'Does it have enough petrol?' my father asked.

'The petrol tank is full.'

As a taxi driver, my father was quite familiar with the common snags with cars. Instead of despairing, he asked Mr Chauhan to open the bonnet. Getting out of the car, he began tinkering with its machinery, his face hidden under the bonnet. With our hands on the window and our mouths open, my mother and I stared helplessly at the car. If my father and Balbir Uncle ran back into the house, it would evoke suspicion. And if they didn't, the mob would close in on them soon. In fact, two or three men had even begun hovering around the car, gazing at the passengers suspiciously.

Shutting the bonnet, my father asked Mr Chauhan to start the engine again. As he turned the key in the ignition, the engine roared to life. Before the men could decide whether they should stop the car, it sped out of the locality.

It was many days later that I learnt what happened subsequently from Balbir Uncle.

As they drove out of Babarpur, Mr Chauhan asked my father, 'Praji, what did you do to get the engine started?'

'The timing belt was loose,' my father replied, 'By god's grace, I managed to fix it in time.'

After covering some distance, they had to take a U-turn as the road to Vivek Vihar was blocked by a heap of drainpipes. My father requested Mr Chauhan to drive them to his relative's house on Pandara Road. Just when the car reached the Sau Foota road, it was flagged down by a mob comprising some twenty-five people. 'Please don't put your life in danger by arguing with the mob,' my father implored to Mr Chauhan. 'If they recognise us, we will get out of the car. Don't make the mistake of defending us or else they will kill you too.'

'Don't worry, Sardarji,' said Mr Chauhan, 'Nothing will happen.'

He craned his neck out of the window. 'We are going to Safdarjung Hospital to visit my ailing mother,' he pleaded with the mob. 'Please let us go. Her condition is very critical.' A few men searched his bag lying on the dashboard. Even as they found a few sachets of medicines, medical papers, food and a water flask in it, they kept gazing at all the four passengers suspiciously. Suddenly, they saw an elderly man in his sixties wading through the crowd. He inspected the inmates of the car closely and ordered the men, 'Let them go.' His voice had such a magical effect on the mob that they dispersed instantly. Some of them even removed the drainpipes from the road. Why did this old man spare them will forever remain a mystery.

Just as the car reached Khajuri Khas, Mr Chauhan pointed at a dozen odd men standing on the left side of the road. The mob directed them to stop the car by waving their lathis. When they didn't halt, the men began throwing stones at the car. 'Drive fast,' my father said to Mr Chauhan. But he was in the habit of driving at a moderate speed. Then some hundred metres away, a mob of twenty men flailed their hands signalling for them to stop. Mr Chauhan kept driving. More stones hit the car. One broke the glass of the front window and ricocheted inside the car. Fortunately, it didn't hit anybody. The other stones landed on the bonnet, the left doors and backside of the car. Balbir Uncle was so worried about Mrs Chauhan that he shielded her head with his hands. Their hearts froze when they saw another mob, a bigger one this time, standing some two metres ahead.

'Let me get behind the wheel,' my father pleaded to Mr Chauhan. 'We need to drive much faster to get out of here.'

'Should I stop?'

'Continue driving.' My father deftly managed to slip into the driving seat from behind Mr Chauhan. The car suddenly accelerated to about ninety kilometres per hour. They noticed there were no mobs on the right side of the road. No traffic either. My father slowed the speed of the car, rammed it on the small divider and got it on the right side of the road. They were now far away from the rioters. The mob could only pelt stones at the speeding car. After driving another kilometre, when they realised that the road on either side was empty, my father brought the car back to the left side. They were soon on the Wazirabad Bridge crossing the Yamuna. As the car sped towards Kashmere Gate, everyone was thanking god for getting them out of the hell and sparing their lives.

Three hours after my father had left, the telephone rang. It was Balbir Uncle calling from Pandara Road. To learn that everybody was safe diminished our anxiety instantly. My mother closed her eyes and sat down on the sofa, utterly exhausted. Since the time my father had left, she hadn't ceased praying.

As Mr Chauhan had feared, a mob comprising about ten men barged into Mr Bains's house that evening. 'Tell the Sikhs to come out,' one of the men hollered at Mr Bains, 'If we find any of them here, we won't spare you.'

'There are no Sikhs here,' screamed Mr Bains, 'It's just me and my family. What makes you think that I'd shelter them?'

After searching the entire house carefully, the mob left quietly. The rioters ran amok in the locality till the night of 3 November, searching, looting and killing.

On 4 November, the Army took control of the violence-affected areas. At the sight of the men in olive green and military vehicles, the mobs dispersed in no time. My father called Mamaji over the telephone and said that he would be sending two cycle rickshaws to his house the next morning to get his and Balbir Uncle's families to Lalaji's house. It was decided that we kids will sit in the first rickshaw while my mother would go to Mr Sharma's house in the second rickshaw to pick up Balbir Uncle's wife, Kulvinder Aunty, and their two sons, aged one and three.

Early in the morning on 5 November, two middle-aged rickshawalas arrived at Mamaji's house. Even though there had been no incidents of violence, Mamaji told the first rickshawala, 'Be careful.'

'Haanji, sahib,' said the rickshawala, 'I will drop the three girls safely. They are like my own daughters.' With his braids, Inderjeet had been mistaken as a girl even by the rickshawala. My mother sat down in the second rickshaw and motioned for her rickshawala to follow us.

I sat in the middle, holding my siblings' hands. Crossing the Sau Foota road, the rickshaw inched towards our house. From a distance, I saw our burnt-down car. My eyes fell on our house: someone had closed its wrought-iron gate. The house, that had been recently white-washed, was covered with black soot now. It looked like a haunted place. After covering some distance, I looked back. My mother's rickshaw had stopped outside Mr Sharma's house. Kulvinder Aunty gave her youngest son to Mother to hold and sat beside my mother with her elder son. Their rickshaw began following us.

There were signs of violence everywhere in the locality. I saw three Sikh homes charred down just like ours. A few Bajaj scooters and another car doused by flames stood on either side of the road. Shards of glass were scattered everywhere. A few metres away, I saw a burnt-down truck. There was a pool of blood on the road and a loose blue turban lying beside the truck. A comb too! All tell-tale signs of the ghastly murder of a Sikh. He must have been the truck's driver.

Except for an Army jeep and an occasional cyclist, the road was completely empty. As we passed by the adjoining Gorakh Park, I suddenly felt a sinking sensation in my stomach. A human hand, with a steel bracelet around it, decapitated from the elbow, lay on the ground. A few metres away was a severed leg. A wrist some distance away and then the torso to which these organs must have belonged. My siblings clutched at me in fear. I could feel their tiny fingers tightening around my hands. I wanted to tell them to close their eyes but felt so nauseated that I couldn't utter a single word.

There was deathly silence all around and all we heard was the movement of the chain, pedals and other parts of the rickety rickshaw. As we passed through Rohtash Nagar, I noticed there were no signs of arson and bloodshed. I learnt later that because of the sizeable number of Sikhs in the locality, the mobs hadn't dared to enter it. Ironically, it was just a month ago that we had left it to live in Babarpur! Was it in our destiny to suffer? To lose everything we had? I often wonder if tragedies in our lives are predestined and we are powerless to sidestep them.

Just before Shahdara Taxi Stand, I saw the showroom of TVs, fridges and washing machines belonging to the Walias, a Sikh family. It had been reduced to ashes. At the taxi stand, we saw the remains of several cars torched by rioters.

At Mansarovar Park, the bodies of about half-a-dozen Sikhs were strewn around. Some bodies had their limbs missing. Some limbs had their body missing. Some bodies were swollen, some charred beyond recognition. Because of the horrific smell—the smell of decaying flesh—the rickshawala covered his nose with his cloth while we squeezed our noses. The bodies must have been lying there for three or four days. And the family members of these dead men might still be waiting for them. Praying to god feverishly to send them back home. Or searching for them in vain.

Soon, we were at the railway crossing. Three more bodies lay beside the railway tracks: the first one was decapitated, the second one was bloated as if filled with air and the third lay with its eyes still open, as if imploring passers-by to help him. The clothes on these bodies were in tatters and blood-soaked. Their limbs had gone stiff and they lay curled up in pitiable angles. Though the rickshawala rode fast, the seven-kilometre journey seemed to go on forever. Even now, it seems surreal. But it had such a powerful effect on me that from then onwards, I find myself least surprised by the barbarities human beings are capable of.

Lalaji and his family greeted us with affection but all three of us were so numb that we could barely respond. Soon Mother, too, arrived with Kulvinder Aunty and her sons. My father and Balbir Uncle, who had reached Lalaji's place the same morning, hugged us kids the moment they saw us.

Balbir Uncle and his family went to live with one of their relatives in Karol Bagh the next day. Father informed us that both our matadors had been torched by the mobs. We had lost our house, car, business, jewellery, clothes, utensils, practically everything we had. Whatever my father had earned till now had been taken away from us in one fell swoop. We were in a state of grieving, the pain of being robbed of our belongings and becoming a target of the mob tugged at our hearts. But Lalaji and his family gave us so much love and hope that it saved my parents from losing their minds. I often heard Lalaji telling them. 'It was a storm and it's gone now. Don't despair. I promise you that everything will be alright. This is your house. Stay here.'

'What if the riots start again?' my father asked Lalaji. 'No, we must now settle in Punjab.'

Lalaji calmed my father down and suggested new ideas to resume his business. He took us kids to the market and got us each a new set of clothes. Sensing my mother's fragile state of mind, Lalaji's wife never left her alone. She encouraged her to talk and even when she was cooking, she would often ask my mother if she needed anything. I was surprised to notice that my mother had suddenly become withdrawn.

A week later, we visited our home in Babarpur. It was completely charred, its doors, windows, and everything the mob couldn't carry, reduced to ash. We found a handful of teaspoons in the kitchen. The mob had also left behind our badminton racquets that we hung on two nails in the drawing room. The fire had twisted them out of shape and the heat had affixed them on to the wall. Just beside the heap of ash, lay a small red cloth, its ends tied together in a knot. Seeing it, my mother's eyes lit up instantly. She picked it up and felt it with her fingers. 'What's that?' my father asked her.

'I can't fathom how the mob didn't notice this,' my mother exclaimed as she handed over the red cloth to my father. 'And why the fire spared it.'

As Father untied the ends of the cloth, he discovered five notes of hundred rupees crumpled inside it. It was little money but we felt so happy to find it. Soon, Mr Aggarwal, Mr Sharma and a few other neighbours arrived. We learnt that out of the seven Sikh families living in our locality, four had perished.

After living with Lalaji for fifteen days, my father took us to his village in Punjab, contemplating settling down there. But we still had our house in Babarpur. Also, my father realised that if he stayed in the village, he won't be able to give good education to his children.

Soon, we returned to Delhi and began living in a room in Rohtash Nagar. The room was located on the terrace of a house, which belonged to my father's friend. We lived there for two months but my father's friend didn't take any rent from us. Instead, he provided us with a few utensils to cook and some woollen clothes to protect ourselves from the cold.

Whenever anybody gave anything to my parents, I often saw a resigned look on their faces. The hands that gave were now forced to take. We didn't even have any money in the bank as Father had spent all his savings to build our house. Moreover, he had to pay back a small loan taken for the house. One day, one of my father's acquaintances, Mr Gurnam Singh, who lived in the neighbouring town of Sonipat, visited us. A sparsely built Sikh in his late thirties, he ran a small transport business. He handed over a jute bag full of clothes and edibles to my mother. 'My wife has sent this for you. Ever since we heard what you went through, we have been very worried about you.'

'By Waheguru's grace, we are all alive,' said my father. 'Many of our neighbours were caught by the mob and killed. I feel scared all the time.' Mr Singh listened to my father patiently, telling him repeatedly not to fear and have faith in god. Then he turned to us kids, talked to us like an equal and inquired when we would be resuming our school. Before leaving, he gave us a packet of sweets. I then saw him slipping a wad of hundred-rupee notes into my father's pocket even as father kept protesting. When he was gone, father counted the money. Three thousand rupees – a decent sum in the early eighties. I couldn't help being struck by this man's concern for us.

Fiercely independent, my father didn't lament for long and got one of the matadors repaired. The money for it was obtained by selling our house. As our house was completely burnt and the buyer realised that we were in a hurry to sell, we got a measly sum for it. My father started driving the matador himself as he couldn't afford a driver now. Soon, he rented a house in Rohtash Nagar and we kids were back in school after a gap of two months.

A few days later, I saw my father feeding sparrows at our new place. 'Can you talk to these sparrows too?' I asked him.

'Not these ones. They don't talk to me.'

'Then don't feed them.' I raised my hand at the sparrows and they flew away in fright.

My father didn't like it and was on the point of rebuking me. Controlling himself, he said to me, 'Don't scare any living being again. It's because of feeding sparrows that our lives were spared.'

I didn't understand what he meant then, but now I know that he was hinting at the law of karma.

Five years later, my father managed to buy a house in Dilshad Garden. A year after that, he came home driving a new Maruti 800. 'Let's go to the gurudwara first,' he said, beaming like a successful manager of a company.

My father encouraged me to study further even though I saw most of my friends getting married even before completing their graduation. In 1995, while I was in the final year at Shyam Lal College, a middle-aged man visited us. My father wasn't at home at that time. Standing at the gate, this man kept looking at me and my siblings as if he knew us. He seemed familiar but I couldn't place him. When my mother saw him, she burst into a loud exclamation of joy. 'Don't you recognise your uncle?' she asked us in disbelief. 'Peripauna karo.'

As we touched his feet one by one, I learnt that he was the same man from Sonipat, who had visited us after the riots. Soon my father arrived and the two friends hugged each other like long-lost brothers. Even though Mr Gurnam Singh was in a hurry to leave, my father forced him to have lunch. Once again, I couldn't help being struck by his kindly face and the compassion in his voice.

A few days later, my mother told me that Mr Singh had proposed the marriage of his elder son to me. A week later, she handed me his son's photograph. The son looked kind and honest like his father. But when I learnt that after completing twelfth class, he was running a medical store in Sonipat, I baulked at the idea of marrying him. Here, I wanted to study further and my father wanted me to marry this small-town boy who hadn't even graduated! As if reading my thoughts, my father said to me. 'I have met the boy. His name is Jaswinder. He seems quite intelligent.'

'But he is just a 10+2 pass! Okay, he has also done a diploma in pharmacy.'

'It's your life, Raj, you decide. All I know is that you cannot judge people from their degrees. Don't forget, I am only a matriculate.'

I mulled over what my father had said and yet I couldn't ignore the difference between our levels of education. At the same time, I couldn't forget the kindness his father had shown to my family after the riots. If his father could reach out to distressed people, his son was likely to be a kind man himself. With every passing day, I found myself thinking about Jaswinder. Sometime later, when my father asked me if I would like to meet Jaswinder once and then decide, I nodded. My father looked quite pleased.

Soon, Jaswinder, accompanied by his parents and a relative, came to our house. After everybody was done with tea and discussing our respective family members, my father said, 'Let the children talk now.' Everybody, including my mother, walked out of the room.

Jaswinder looked relaxed and even confident. 'You are more educated than I am,' he began, 'If you don't like it, please let me know. I will say no to my father.'

'Do you handle the medical shop independently?' I asked him.

'I have two assistants,' he replied. Then, somewhat shyly, he added, 'I have also applied for the entrance exam for a bachelor's course in physiotherapy. If I get through, I will study. Looking at you, I feel inspired to study further.'

'I would like to complete my MSc,' I informed him.

'That's a good idea!' he exclaimed.

My father had said that Jaswinder was intelligent. I also found him quite understanding. In a month's time, we were sort of engaged. There was no ceremony, only our parents said yes to each other. It was decided that we would marry after completing our education. Jaswinder cleared the entrance test, while I enrolled in the MSc course a year later. Four years later, when we got married, Jaswinder was a practising physiotherapist, while I was teaching maths in a public school in Delhi. After our wedding, I shifted to Sonipat and began teaching in a school there. We now have two kids and I must say that marrying Jaswinder has been the best decision of my life. I don't think I would have found a better man.

Now seventy-one, my father is still running his business.

Only now, instead of matadors, he has a fleet of buses. My sister is married to an engineer and my brother is a sales manager at a multinational company. We avoid talking about the riots as they trigger distressing memories. We also avoid the subject because of my mother. The trauma of the riots has impacted her so severely that whenever she talks about those days, she usually ends up fainting after some time.

It was many years after the riots that she told us that while coming back from Mr Bains's house after warning Father, she saw Mr Gurdev Singh, a Sikh who lived in our neighbourhood, pulled down from his scooter by the mob and burnt alive. 'When the mob began hitting him with iron rods, his turban fell off his head and his screams rent the air. He looked at me with pleading eyes. As if I would do something to rescue him. What could I have done?' my mother choked, fighting her tears. 'Had I interfered, the mob would have killed me too. As the men doused him with kerosene oil, he kept pleading with them to let him go to his wife and children. "Main ki kitta?" he questioned them repeatedly but the mob didn't leave him. When a man lit him with a matchstick and flames leapt from his body, he ran around the circle of men pleading with them to put out the fire. His plaintive cries became dreadful. It would have been much better to die than to witness this spectacle. He was engulfed in flames: right from his head to his legs. He was screaming so hysterically that I could hear him crying both while inhaling and exhaling. He ran amok. His hands flailing. His legs hitting the ground with such force that you could feel the vibrations a few feet away. Then he fell down. Howling. And rolling on the ground to get rid of the flames. But his clothes were drenched in kerosene. The mob looked at him impassively. His cries still haunt me, puttar, his cries still haunt me!'

Weeping inconsolably, my mother fainted soon after. We have taken her to several psychiatrists but it has been of little help. Some say that she is suffering from Post-Traumatic Stress Disorder (PTSD). It's an environmental shock that changes the brain and it's not known if it's reversible. Other psychiatrists have tried to treat her with different medicines, but they have soon realised how ineffective they are. They now say that the only cure is time. Time? Thirty-two years have passed. How much more time will my mother need to recover? She has almost forgotten to laugh and speaks so little.

For several years after the riots, I found myself asking god every day why we had to suffer. On the other hand, I had found my father quite composed, as if nothing had happened. One day, I confronted him, 'Why is it that you have no anger for anybody despite what we went through?'

'What's the point in being angry and hurting myself? The ways of life are mysterious, Raj. I don't know why we have to suffer. But sometimes, our sufferings can lead us to something important—it could be a crucial lesson or a change for the better—we just can't anticipate.'

'What does that mean?' I asked, feeling confused by his words.

'Haven't you thought,' he looked at me fixedly, 'that because of the riots, Mr Gurnam Singh visited us? And it led to your marriage with Jaswinder. Who could have imagined that?' After a short pause, he added, 'The riots also taught me that one shouldn't give up even in a hopeless situation. Look, I was able to rebuild our lives from scratch. We are all capable of achieving much more than what we expect from ourselves.'

It was evening and Father took me to the terrace of our house. I saw him filling water in a shallow tumbler and scattering grains of millet in a corner. A few sparrows suddenly came from nowhere and began twittering excitedly as if happy to see this caring elderly man. 'Do you still talk to them?' I asked my father. He broke into a loud guffaw.

About the Contributors

Kirpal Dhillon is former Director General of Police, Punjab and Madhya Pradesh as well as vice chancellor of Bhopal University. A fellow of IIAS, Shimla, he has written four books: *Defenders of the Establishment, Police and Politics in India, Identity and Survival: Sikh Militancy in India* and *Time Present and Time Past: Memoirs of a Top Cop.* In addition, several Indian and foreign anthologies carry his essays. Described as 'the world's foremost historian of South Asian criminal justice systems' in a recent US publication, *The Locust Effect,* by Gary Haugin, Dhillon is a familiar figure at international conferences

Ajeet Cour is a well-known Punjabi fiction writer and author of several novels and collections of short stories. Her works have been widely translated into quite a few Indian and foreign languages. She is the recipient of many national and international awards, including the Sahitya Akademi Award and the Padma Shri. She is one of thc '1000 Women Peace Crusaders Across the Globe' for the Collective Nobel Peace Prize. Ajeet founded the Foundation of SAARC Writers and Literature, and the Academy of Fine Arts and Literature, a cultural centre in Siri

Fort in 1975. She also initiated the idea of cultural connectivity among the SAARC countries for peace way back in 1986. Her cultural institution has three museums and a free library. It also organises cultural gatherings, poetry readings, and art exhibitions throughout the year.

Satjit Wadva is an author and translator. Her books include *Understanding Guru Granth Sahib: The Living Guru, Guru Nanak: The Singer Divine,* and *Understanding Japjee Sahib: The Essence of Guru Granth Sahib* among many others.

Rizio Yohannan Raj is a bilingual writer, educationist, and governance thinker. She is the founder and executive director of the cultural think-space LILA Foundation for Translocal Initiatives (www.lilafoundation.in), and creative director of ILF Samanvay, the Indian Languages Festival. Her engagement and mediation with ideas and words are aimed at initiating and driving a politico-aesthetic discourse relevant to the times and charged with transformative content.

Hartosh Singh Bal is currently working on a book on the 1984 Sikh massacres. He is the author of a travelogue set along the Narmada river, *Waters Close Over Us,* and is co-author of *A Certain Ambiguity: A Mathematical Novel.*

Preeti Gill is an independent editor and literary agent who has been part of the publishing industry for more than twenty years. She was the senior commissioning editor and rights director at Kali for Women and Zubaan, an independent feminist press. She has worked extensively on issues of conflict and women in the

Northeast of India and has edited a volume of non-fiction essays on the region called *The Peripheral Centre: Voices from India's Northeast.* She is also co-editor along with Sanjoy Hazarika of *Bearing Witness: A Report on the Impact of Conflict on Women in Nagaland and Assam* and co-editor along with Uma Chakravarty of *Shadow Lives: Widowhood in India.*

Humra Quraishi is a Delhi-based writer, columnist and journalist. Her books include *Kashmir: The Untold Story, Views: Yours and Mine, More Bad Time Tales, Divine Legacy: Dagars & Dhrupad* and *Meer.* With the late Khushwant Singh, she has co-authored *The Good, the Bad and the Ridiculous: Profiles, Absolute Khushwant* and a series of other writings. Her take on what's it like to be a singleton in today's turbulent times is part of the anthology *Chasing the Good Life: On Being Single.* And one of her essays, *The State Can't Snatch Away our Children* is part of the anthology *Of Mothers And Others.* Her short stories have been published in several magazines and journals.

Rana Chhina served in the Indian Air Force as a helicopter pilot and is a recipient of the Macgregor Medal for best military reconnaissance in 1986. He is currently Secretary and Editor of the United Service Institution of India Centre for Armed Forces Historical Research and Vice President of the Indian Military Historical Society, UK. He is a member of the IAF Aerospace Museum's Apex Steering Committee and the Government of India's Archival Advisory Board, as well as the joint USI-MEA Steering Committee responsible for coordinating international and national commemoration of India's participation in the First World War in connection with the centenary of the conflict.

NS Madhavan is an acclaimed and popular contemporary writer of Malayalam novels, short stories and essays. Many of his works have been translated into English. 'When Big Trees Fall' was originally published in Malayalam in 2004. It was later adapted into an award-winning motion picture tiled 'Kaya Taran'.

Dramaturge and socio-political commentator, **NP Ashley** is assistant professor of English and coordinator of Centre for Translations at St Stephen's College, New Delhi. He has translated stories by Saadat Hasan Manto and O Henry, and articles by Amitav Ghosh and Mukul Kesavan into Malayalam.

Jaspreet Singh is the author of two novels, *Helium* and *Chef*, and a collection of short stories titled *Seventeen Tomatoes: Tales from Kashmir*. He has also published a number of essays.

Mridula Garg is the winner of the Sahitya Akademi Award and the Vyas Samman. She has published eight novels and ninety stories in Hindi apart from plays, travelogues and essays. Three novels, *Chittacobra, Anitya* (*Halfway to Nowhere*) and *Kathgulab* (*Country of Goodbyes*) and many stories have been translated into German, Russian, Japanese, Italian, and Czech, apart from English. *Chittacobra, Anitya* and some stories were translated into English by the author herself. She carries a wry sense of humour and serious self-reflection into her work with equal ease.

Vikram Kapur is the author of two novels. His short fiction and nonfiction have been published widely in India and abroad. His short stories have been shortlisted for major international prizes including, among others, the Commonwealth Short Story Prize and broadcast over the radio. His latest novel will be published in the coming year. Vikram is currently an associate professor of English at Shiv Nadar University.

Pratyaksha is an award-winning author of three books of short stories in Hindi – *Jungle ka Jadootiltil, Pahardopahar Thumri* and *Ek Din Marrakech,* and an English anthology of short stories entitled *Rainsong*. Her English novella *Meet me Tomorrow* was published in 2016. In addition, she is a published poet and a painter whose work has appeared in *The Four Quarters Magazine*. She blogs at www.pratyaksha.blogspot.com

Harish Narang is a former professor of English from Jawaharlal Nehru University, New Delhi. He writes stories in Hindi and English. He has written two short-story collections in Hindi titled *Pakistani Baccha* and *Sunte the Sahar Hogi.* He is also a translator, with *Manto My Love* being the latest of over twenty books that have been translated by him.

Aditya Sharma studied Law at Delhi University and then practised in his hometown for a couple of years – until he discovered he wanted to be a writer. He started off by freelancing for several national newspapers and magazines. When a weekly publication took him on as a journalist in Delhi, he was more than relieved to be rescued from a lawyer's drab life in the district courts. He has since then worked with several magazines including the *Reader's Digest* and also written for *The Hindu, The Tribune, Sahara Time* and *Life Positive*. A Mumbai-based writer, *Champs of Devgarh* is his first novel.

Acknowledgements

A book begins as an idea in its creator's head, but it takes the efforts of several individuals to turn that idea into a book. Rashmi Menon, Manoj Kulkarni and Vikas Rakheja at Amaryllis had the foresight to commission the book. The contributors believed in the idea and came forward to contribute with passion, helping turn a mere idea into tangible words and pages. Some of them did more than just contribute. They were kind enough to introduce me to other contributors. Ms Neha Mishra, my graduate assistant at Shiv Nadar University, burnt a lot of midnight oil tirelessly proofreading the final drafts of the various contributions. And, finally, my employers at Shiv Nadar University, who have supported me in my creative pursuits. I thank you all.